THE LETTERS OF MAYO LIND

Thanks to Lind's letters, the men who went to the front are not cold strangers left yellowing in black and white photos taken in that period. They are real, living, breathing, joking and honest young men with familiar sounding names from the bays and outports and St. John's.

—Craig Westcott, *The Newfoundland Herald*

Lind's letters home make a fascinating book. His account of life as a Newfoundland soldier fighting in the Great War brings us to a better understanding of what it was like in the training camps and trenches.

—Mike McCarthy, *The Telegram*, St. John's

GW00535867

THE CHILDHOOD HOME OF FRANK LIND, AT LITTLE BAY.

Frank is seen standing between the twisted birch tree and the window. His position is marked by a cross.

THE LETTERS
OF
MAYO LIND

**Newfoundland's Unofficial War Correspondent
1914-1916**

With an Introduction (1919)
by J. ALEX. ROBINSON, LL.D.
Formerly Editor of the Daily News
and
A Foreword (2001)
by Peter Neary

Originally published by
Robinson & Co., Limited, print
1919

St. John's, Newfoundland
2001

© 2001, Creative Book Publishing

Le Conseil des Arts | The Canada Council
du Canada | for the Arts

We acknowledge the support of The Canada Council for the Arts
for our publishing program.

We acknowledge the financial support of the Government of Canada through the
Book Publishing Industry Development Program (BPIDP) for our publishing actvities.

As far as is possible, this book is a faithful reproduction of the original text as written
by Francis T. (Mayo) Lind in 1914 to 1916, and subsequently published in book
form by Robinson & Co., Limited, in 1919. The book has been completely reset and
formatted to current standards, without compromising the thoughts expressed by its
author. The only substantive addition to the text is the foreword by Peter Neary,
Professor of History, The University of Western Ontario. Any requests for photo-
copying, recording, taping or information storage and retrieval systems of any part of
this publication of *The Letters of Mayo Lind* shall be directed in writing to the Canadian
Reprography Collective, One Yonge Street, Suite 1900, Toronto, Ontario M5E 1E5.

∞ Printed on acid-free paper

Cover design by Joanne Snook-Hann

Published by KILLICK PRESS (an imprint of CREATIVE BOOK PUBLISHING)
a division of 10366 Newfoundland Limited
a Robinson-Blackmore Printing & Publishing associated company
P.O. Box 8660, St. John's, Newfoundland A1B 3T7
Second Printiong (this edition) November 2001

Printed in Canada by:
ROBINSON-BLACKMORE PRINTING & PUBLISHING

Canadian Cataloguing in Publication Data

Lind, Francis T. (Francis Thomas), 1879-1916

The letters of Mayo Lind: Newfoundland's unofficial war
correspondent, 1914-1916

Includes index.

Reprint of ed. published: St. John's, Nfld. : Robinson & Co., 1919.

ISBN 1-894294-30-0

1. Lind, Francis T. (Francis Thomas), 1879-1916—Correspondence. 2. Great
Britian. Army. Newfoundland Regiment, 1st. 3. World War, 1914-1918—Personal
narratives, Canadian.   4. War correspondents—Newfoundland—Correspondence.
5. Newfoundlanders—Correspondence.   I. Title

D640.L48 2001   940.4'81718   C2001-900434-6

Victor yet in his grave
All that he had he gave;
Nor may we weep for the might-have-been,
For the quenchless flame of a heart aglow
Burns clear that the soul yet blind may know
The vision splendid his eyes have seen.

Weep but the wasted life
Of him who shrinks from the strife,
Shunning the path that the brave have trod,
Not for the friend whose task is done
Who strove, with his face to the morning sun,
Up and up to his God!

FOREWORD

ORLD WAR I, known to the generation that lived through it as the Great War, shaped the history of the twentieth century. In the Allied countries, the conflict began in August 1914 with a rush of patriotism and the expectation that the fighting would be brief. Victory, it was believed, was but a few weeks or months away. It would all be over by Christmas. This optimistic forecast, along with much else, was soon shattered by terrible events. Instead of being short and glorious, the war turned out to be long and unremitting. In France, the contest quickly degenerated into trench warfare, a savage form of combat that tested the resolve of the rival armies and produced casualties on a hitherto unimaginable scale. As death and destruction piled upon death and destruction, there seemed to be no way out, until, finally, the Allies were able to gain the advantage and force surrender.

The Armistice that took effect on the eleventh hour of the eleventh day of the eleventh month of 1918 was celebrated on the Allied side as the final act of a great military triumph, but in truth it was a merciful deliverance. On the general service medal issued to members of the British forces after the war were inscribed the words "The Great War for Civilisation 1914-1919." The sentiment thus expressed was both understandable and noble, but it belied a bitter and divisive legacy that cast a long shadow over the remainder of the century. The seeds of World War II (1939-45) were sown in the hard peace agreement made with Germany in 1919. And the seeds of the Cold War that followed World War II were sown in the 1917 Bolshevik revolution in Russia, which was itself triggered by the catastrophic military reverses suffered by the Czarist government on the bloody Eastern Front during the Great War.

Newfoundland was connected to these epic world events through membership in the British Empire. When the United Kingdom went to war in August 1914, Newfoundland was automatically at war, and Newfoundlanders quickly rallied to the cause of the mother country. First to be called up were members of the Royal Naval Reserve, many of whom were overseas before the end of 1914. By this time the government of Newfoundland had also organized a regiment. Recruitment for this force, which was trained at Pleasantville, began after a proclamation was issued by the Governor on 21 August. The first members of the Newfoundland Regiment (from 1917 the Royal Newfoundland Regiment) to go overseas left St. John's for the United Kingdom in October. This contingent constituted the "First Five Hundred," known as the Blue Puttees. The Newfoundland Regiment subsequently served in the slogging Gallipoli campaign and in the trenches of France. According to the best estimate of the historian David Parsons, of 790 members of the regiment (officers and men) who went over the top at Beaumont Hamel on I July 1916, the opening day of the Battle of the Somme, "272 were killed, died of wounds or were missing and presumed dead" and another 438 were wounded. This was a staggering total of 710, and it made Beaumont Hamel the defining event in Newfoundland's military participation in the Great War.

On the home front, the war brought a wave of social and economic change. In time, the conflict produced deep political divisions, but it also rallied Newfoundlanders across denominational lines and fostered new causes and institutions with broad popular appeal. The war also gave Newfoundlanders a new group of national heroes. Prominent among these were Tommy Ricketts (winner of the Victoria Cross), the diarist Owen Steele (who died following Beaumont Hamel), and Gerald ("Jerry") Whitty (who won the Military Cross and was later Dominion Secretary of the Great War Veterans' Association).

Francis ("Frank") T. Lind, the author of the memorable work reprinted here, belongs with this select company. His letters home, originally published in the St. John's *Daily News* and then collected in book form in 1919 (with a poignant introduction by the newspaperman J. Alexander Robinson), gave Newfoundlanders a graphic and compelling account of day-to-day regimental life overseas and of the vicissitudes of war. Lind acquired the nickname Mayo after noting in his letter of 20 May 1915 that good tobacco was "almost impossible to get" in Scotland and that "a stick of 'Mayo'" — a product of Imperial Tobacco, St. John's — was "indeed a luxury." A supply of "Mayo-Linds" was soon dispatched from Newfoundland to the men overseas, and thereafter Lind was affectionately known as Mayo. When he was listed among the fallen at Beaumont Hamel, Newfoundlanders lost not only a gallant soldier but a talented literary voice. His letters remain indispensable reading for anyone who seeks to understand Newfoundland's role in the Great War,

In 2014 there is bound to be a fresh remembrance of the terrible 1914-18 war. Newfoundlanders are indeed fortunate that in preparation for the centenary, which will, no doubt, occasion a flood of historical writing and revisionist interpretation, the Royal Newfoundland Regiment has seen fit to reissue *The Letters of Mayo Lind*, in memory of Lind and his generation. The book is being reissued on 1 July 2001 to coincide with the eighty-fifth anniversary of Beaumont Hamel and the opening of an. interpretation centre there by the Government of Canada. Mayo Lind's prose remains fresh and vigorous, and his words bring back a time that should not be forgotten. His letters have not grown old, and they deserve to be read by a new generation of his compatriots.

Peter Neary
Professor of History
The University of Western Ontario
January 2001

INTRODUCTION

RIVATE FRANCIS T. LIND — Mayo-Lind as he is so well known to Newfoundlanders — was born at Bett's Cove, Notre Dame Bay, on March 9th, 1879. There and at Little Bay Mines he received his education. At the age of fourteen he entered the employ of J.W. Hodge of Fogo, where he was engaged for a few years. From Fogo he came to St. John's, joining the staff of Ayre & Sons, Ltd. Later he went to Amherst, Nova Scotia, where he was employed in the office of Rhodes and Curry, Ltd. On returning to St. John's he resumed his former position at Ayre & Sons, Ltd. Shortly afterwards he entered the employ of Earle, Sons & Co. at Fogo, where on Sept. 16th, 1914, with his friend and colleague, Jack Brett, now of the G.P.O., and five others, he enlisted. When the call to the colours came, Frank was over thirty-fiveyears of age and entitled to moral exemption, but the Old Grey Mother needed him, there were wrongs to be righted, foes to overcome, evils to be uprooted, justice to be done, and the young man hastened to do his part, rejoicing in the vigour of body and mind which enabled him to play a man's part in the greatest crisis of the centuries. The Empire is justly proud of the millions of her sons who hesitated not and lingered not.

As a soldier Frank Lind shared in the honours and the glory of service with thousands of others. Like them he did his duty fearlessly and zealously, and with hundreds of Newfoundland's honoured sons fell gallantly on the field of Beaumont Hamel, heroes unsung and undecorated, but heroes who

FRANCIS THOMAS LIND
"MAYO LIND"

maintained the honour of their Island home, and with others, who fought and fell on a thousand battlefields, assured to Newfoundland her safety, to the Empire its integrity, and to the world its freedom.

Frank Lind had no training in journalism; he was not familiar with the editorial sanctum or the publishing office. Possibly therein lies the charm of his letters. They are the unstudied expressions of an observant man in the maturity of his early manhood, written with one thought only, to bring

REV. HENRY LIND
Rural Dean of St. George's

comfort and confidence to those in his far off native land, whose boys were sharing with him the experiences of camp life, and the dangers of Gallipoli and France. His letters were written in tents and on boats, in YMCA Huts, and wayside estaminets; some of them were penned in rest billets, and others in the trenches amid the ominous discords of shell and shrapnel. It may be that ancestry had some share in the making of Newfoundland's First War Correspondent.

Frank Lind was the fifth son of the late Henry Lind, for many years paymaster at Little Bay Mines, and a grandson of the Rev. Henry Lind, a native of London, England. Mr. and Mrs. Lind came to Newfoundland about 1829. An extract from the report of the "Society for Educating the Poor of Newfoundland, 1828-1829," reads:

> It will be the "duty of the successors of your present committee to dismiss very shortly to Newfoundland five new teachers, viz., Mr. and Mrs. Meek, Mr. and Mrs. Lind and Mr. "Walker."

The report for the following year, referring to the eagerness of the people of Port de Grave to secure a teacher, says:

> Under these circumstances he (Mr. Willoughby) considered it advisable to change the proposed destination of Mr. and Mrs. Lind from Twillingate (where the school house was not in so forward a state) to Port de Grave. A highly satisfactory letter has been received from Mr. Lind, by which it appears that he and Mrs. Lind had as many scholars as they were able to accommodate, and that very many more were obliged to wait till the rooms were completed.

The report for 1842-43 states that of the principal teachers sent out from England nine had received ordination, of whom three had been transferred to the Society for the Propagation of the Gospel. Thus after ten years of faithful service as a teacher, service in which his wife had faithfully and devotedly

MRS. CAROLINE LIND
Grandmother of Frank

shared, the young Englishman was ordained in 1840 by the late Bishop Spencer, and two years later was raised by him to priesthood. His first mission was at Catalina. The following year, 1841, Mr. Lind was transferred to Heart's Content, where he remained in labours abundant for sixteen years. In 1857 the Rev. Henry Lind was appointed Rural Dean of Bay St. George where he died in 1869 after twelve years of faithful and zealous service, leaving two children, Henry, father of Frank Lind, and Caroline. Henry was born at Port de Grave on Nov. 21st, 1832, and died at Little Bay, Notre Dame Bay, on February 29, 1908. The wife of the Rural Dean, moved to Halifax after her husband's death and subsequently to Boston, where she died.

Henry Lind, father of Frank, married Elizabeth Walker, daughter of the late John Walker of St. John's, whose father was a well-known ships' carpenter and a native of Scotland. Frank's mother, who resides with her son, J.M. Lind, at Little Bay, was born at Scilly Cove, now known as Winterton, in Trinity Bay, in 1846, five months after the Great Fire, in which her father, John Walker lost all his property. Her mother was a daughter of Robert Hiscock, probably of Winterton or its vicinity. Thus in the veins of the young soldier-correspondent coursed the blood of English, Scottish and Newfoundland sires. With such a heritage it is not difficult to discover whence came the sturdy loyalty, the kindly courtesy, the refreshing humour, and the indomitable spirit which characterized Mayo Lind.

Like his ancestry, so his immediate family connections are cosmopolitan. One brother, H.J. Lind, is now at Grand Falls, another, J.M. Lind, is doing business at Little Bay; a third, W.H. Lind, is pay-master with the Dominion Coal Company, Cape Breton, whilst R.G. Lind, the fourth of the five brothers, resides in the United States. Amongst the relatives are or were, the late E.G. Lind, a well-known architect of Wilmington, Delaware; William Murdoch Lind, a New York Journalist, Dr. E. George Lind, Chief Fiscal Officer of the United States Reclamation Service at Washington and Arthur M. Lind, architect, in North Dakota.

JOHN WALKER
Grandfather of Frank

A cousin, Robert Walker, joined a Canadian regiment, winning the Military Medal, at the cost of his foot and many wounds, only two of his platoon escaping, the officer and himself. The former received the Victoria Cross. Another cousin, Jenny Walker, joined the Red Cross for Overseas, and was in charge of a camp in the United States. A nephew, now in Grand Falls, made persistent efforts to serve his King and Country and to avenge his uncle's death, and when repeated applications met with unfavourable response from the Medical Board, volunteered for the Air Force, but without success.

Whilst to the student of heredity, family details of this character may not be without value, to the readers of.Frank Lind's letters in the *Daily News* they will be of real interest, for the name of the young soldier, who received his baptism of journalism, as well as of fire, amid the comradeship of Newfoundland's brave and generous soldier sons, has long been a household word in the homes that rear their hospitable walls along our six thousand miles of coastline or in our inland towns.

Francis Lind was a soldier for less than two years, but with those hundreds of gallant and glorious lads at Beaumont Hamel he proudly and fearlessly shared in vicarious sacrifice. He was a journalist for little more than eighteen months but by his cheerful, hopeful, helpful letters he won for himself the gratitude and affection of hundreds of anxious hearts.

It was not my privilege to know Frank Lind personally, just as it was not that of the thousands of *Daily News*' readers to whom his letters brought courage and cheer. And yet none is better known in Newfoundland today than this young soldier-writer. His letters reveal his personality. For his comrades and colleagues he has nothing but praise. There is a spirit of loyalty which is peculiarly precious in these days of self advertisement. It is unreasonable to suppose that the young soldier met with none but friends and saw nothing but the kindly side of life and mingled only with the genial and the joyous; but from first to last there was never an unkind criticism. He is unsparing in appreciation and praise. Where none is possible he is silent. Frank Lind learned in his comparative youth what it too often takes the mellowing influences of life's later years to teach. Perhaps that is why Newfoundland holds his memory in affection, and why in many homes in city and outport Frank Lind's name is received as that of an intimate and personal friend.

Corporal Gallishaw, a Newfoundlander who heard the Mother's call when a student at Harvard University, and promptly left the academic halls to join the Home Regiment, pays a charming and merited tribute to Frank Lind in his "Trenching at Gallipoli."

"Just about an hour before my turn to watch," he says,

I was suddenly stricken by the fever that lurks in the Peninsula. In the Army no man is sick unless so pronounced by the medical officer. Each morning at nine there is a sick parade. A man taken ill after that has to wait until the next morning, and is officially unfit for duty. My turn came at eleven o'clock at night. The man I was to relieve was Frank Lind. He went on at nine. When eleven o'clock came, I was burning up with fever. Lind would not hear of my being roused to relieve him, but continued on the parapet until one o'clock although in that part of the trench snipers had been doing a lot of execution. Then he rested for a couple of hours and at three o'clock resumed his place on the parapet for the remainder of the night. At daybreak he was still there. I slept all through the night, exhausted by the fever and it was not till a few days after that someone else told me what Lind had done. From him I heard no mention of it. Whenever somebody says that war serves only to bring out the worst in a man I think of Frank Lind.

To those who read Frank Lind's letters the tribute will cause no surprise. Men may write what they neither believe nor practice, but there is a transparency in the letters of Mayo Lind through which it is easy to see the man himself, kind, generous, self-sacrificing, modest and sensitive, the kind of man who is content to find his reward in his work, who does kind actions habitually not for gratitude or praise but as a matter of duty. Gallishaw's tribute to Lind comes from one gallant soldier to another.

Frank Lind has been referred to as sensitive. It is curious how closely bravery and modesty are entwined. A man who will march fearlessly across the battlefield, facing, without flinching, storms of shot and shell, will shrink from notoriety or fame. But a soldier has a duty to his comrades as well as to his country. It was with reluctance but under a compelling sense of duty that reference was made by him to the appalling conditions on the Peninsula. Mail after mail brought news of the socks and shirts and comforts prepared in the homes and halls of the land they loved, but day after day passed amid privations and discomforts as unnecessary as they were undeserved. They saw the New Zealanders and Australians, thousands of miles away from their Homeland fully supplied with gifts from home, and it was to the kindness of their Antipodean chums were due all the little luxuries and many of the actual necessaries which were theirs. It was in simple justice to his comrades that the soldier-writer told in well guarded and brief sentences of the true state of affairs on Gallipoli Peninsula. He had the satisfaction of knowing that his exposure and appeal had not been in vain and that despite the unkind comments of a few, the many were grateful and that his letters were mainly instrumental in preventing a repetition of the shameful story of negligence. Where all the responsibility belonged only those within the inner circles know, and it would advantage neither the heroic young soldier nor his comrades to make further inquisition. Probably it may have been shared by many. It will be sufficient to say that to a man whose temperament was ever sloping upon the sunny side there was nothing so uncongenial as throwing shadows athwart the sky. All the brave boys were grateful to the devoted women of Newfoundland who were assiduously toiling for their comfort, and these in their turn were grateful to Frank Lind whose brief recital put a speedy termination to the vexations and incomprehensible delays that had resulted in sufferings that had been so long and patiently borne. It was on a bed of sickness when suffering from the fever that Galipoli had bequeathed to him as a parting legacy, that Frank Lind read the published criticisms of his motives. Private letters show how acutely he felt the injustice and unkindness of the writers. Happily the gallant soldier lived long enough to know how few were those who condemned and how many and how grateful were the mothers and fathers, wives and sweethearts, as well as those true-hearted and patriotic women, whose untiring efforts for the brave lads had been, up to that time, largely nullified by red-tape and inefficiency.

On June 29th, 1916, Frank Lind penned his last letter. "We are out to billets again for a short rest returning to trenches to-morrow, and then ————." What was to be faced within a few brief hours he knew well. Each lad in the regiment, and in the whole 29th Division was aware that stupendous operations were in contemplation. If all went well there were grave dangers to be faced and ultimate triumph to be won. If things went wrong, there would be increased dangers, and greater difficulties, but of defeat none ever dreamed. "And then ———— but never mind that now." It was thus that many a brave fellow peered into the future on those anxious days that preceded Beaumont Hamel's heroic advance. Frank Lind's last letters are his best. The same cheerful spirit pervades all, but as the testing time approached his was a wider vision. He had made tryst with death too often to fear the meeting, and asked the question that doubtless many thousands were asking, knowing full well that the answer might be given within a few brief hours. But calmly he put pen to paper and there within the sound of the guns and with the knowledge that the great struggle was at hand, he told the story which Newfoundlanders were not to read until the writer with so many of the flower of the Old Colony's manhood had been enrolled in the glorious army of soldiers, faithful unto death, to whom the gates of immortality have been opened by the golden keys of service and of sacrifice.

Frank Lind's last letter ends with the familiar words, "With kind regards." It was with kind regards he gazed on his loved native land, his comrades in camp and billet and trench, and in kind regard his memory will be held in Newfoundland by the thousands who have read his letters, and to whom the tidings that Frank Lind's was one amongst the heroic souls that winged their flight from Beaumont Hamel's fateful field, brought both sorrow and pride. It had been the writer's hope to have spent some years of comradeship with the gifted soldier-journalist, amid familiar surroundings. It has been willed otherwise. In memory of the cheerful soldier *The Letters of Mayo Lind* are now presented.

J. ALEX. ROBINSON
St. John's, May 1, 1919

THE LETTERS
of MAYO LIND

THE LETTERS OF MAYO LIND

FIRST LETTER

Fort George,
Inverness-shire, Scotland,
December 26th, 1914.

E ARRIVED AT FORT GEORGE on Dec. 8th, and on landing at Ardeseir, less than two miles from here, a band from the Seaforths was waiting for us, and played the grand old "Soldiers of the King" and, on the march in, the music dropped into Tipperary. We swung along then in good style, but on entering the Fort the band played "The Maple Leaf." They did not seem to know that Newfoundland is NOT Canada, but they thoroughly understand now that we are Newfoundlanders, NOT Canadians. Everywhere in England we were taken as Canadians, and they would favour us with the "Maple Leaf," when what we wanted to hear was the "Banks of Newfoundland," "The Boy in the Gap," or even James Murphy's "Song of the Apples." Now, however, they know us as Newfoundlanders, and are even arranging patriotic airs suitable to dear old Terra Nova.

Nairn, another town (10,000), is seven miles from here. Motor cars are running forth and back all the time. We go there often, as it is only eighteen minutes' run. The people are more than kind to us and cannot do enough to make us happy. Inverness, twelve miles from here (28,000) is a beautiful place, and the same kind attention is shown to us there. Everywhere it is the same. People can't do enough for us, and on going in to visit the people, nine cases out of ten we find the mother or daughter knitting socks or comforts, for the soldiers. We were treated well in England, but nothing can exceed the kindness of the Scotch people. Give me dear old Scotland after this.

This Fort was built in 1763, and is very interesting. The Battle of Culloden was fought just here, and there are so many interesting relics all around us.

The boys are invited to the different towns to teas, etc., and about half the regiment will spend New Year's Day amongst the people they have met. They ask us on sight. The word "1st Newfoundland" seems to bear a charm. I was in Nairn on Christmas Eve, and going down High Street with a chum, we met two children, who inquired: "Are you from Newfoundland?" (don't forget the accent on the second syllable).

We said, "Yes."

They replied, "Well, father and mother want you to come to tea."

We went and thoroughly enjoyed ourselves. This is one instance of many.

Talking about Christmas, well let me tell you about our

Christmas dinner. But here words fail me. It was a repast fit for a king. Lord Brassey and the Anglo-Newfoundland Development Company gave the dinner for the 1st. Newfoundland Regiment, and we did enjoy it. First we had goose, roast of beef, cabbage, potatoes, turnips, etc., then plum pudding and tea, followed by oranges, apples, nuts, raisins, and for a "chaser" they gave us cigarettes (all presented). The puddings were given by Mr. and Mrs. W. Martin formerly of St. John's. You see we are 14 men in each room, and you can imagine the sight as we all sat around the table fairly groaning (the table, not us) with the good things, and the flags of Britain, Russia, France and Belgium hanging all around. The critical time came when Pte. Geo. S. Knight, who was orderly that day, carved the goose, then we all began, and after dinner we had speeches and songs.

PROGRAMME.

Opening Chorus, "Kaiser Bill, the Murderer" — by the Company.

Speech, "Matrimony" — Pte. Thomas Rogers.

Stump Speech, "War in the Air" — Pte. W. Kearley.

Reading, "Who's What" — Pte. Alan Moyes.

Recitation, "The Face on the Bar-room Floor" — Pte. G. S. Knight.

Recitation, "The Lion at Hogan's — Pte. M. O'Neil.

Song (comic) "From the Canteen to the Guard Room" — Pte. J. Cleary.

Stump Speech, "Chocolates Please" — Pte. Wilf Harvey.

Song, "Stop that Talking" — Pte. J. Dunphy.
Instrumental duet — Pte. M. Myler and Pte. Wilf Harvey.
Song, "Kelligrew's Soiree" — Pte. R. Voisey.
Recitation, "Who Broke the Shelf" — Pte. F. Lind.
Speech, "Edinburgh" — Pte. A.M. Pratt.
Song, "Bonnie Scotland" — L.-Corpl. E. Hoare.

GOD SAVE THE KING.

A concert in the Barracks Theatre followed and proved a decided success.

SECOND LETTER

Fort George,
Inverness-shire, Scotland,
Feb. 3rd, 1915.

 HEN LAST I WROTE we were in the midst of our Christmas celebrations, I have also to refer to our Christmas presents from the dear friends left behind, shall we ever forget them for their kindness? There was no end to the good things we received, sweaters, socks and mufflers, cakes and fruit — and to use the words of Brayley's Almanack ads — "other articles too numerous to mention." We feel so grateful to the good people of dear old Terra Nova. Won't we all do our best to show our appreciation, and you can bet that the Newfoundland Boys will not be behind when the opportunity arises. Somebody said (somebody is always saying something) that probably we would not go to the front, but be kept for home defence. Of course we all laughed and took it for a joke, but the thought struck some of us, "supposing such should be the case," but, hush! don't anybody ever dare to hint seriously to any of the First Newfoundland Regiment that they are not going to the front, for I am afraid the result would be

7

very bad, for we are all set on going and want to be in at the finish, and don't you think we would "keep up our end of the plank?" If you doubt it we suggest a trip to Fort George. Watch us on parade, on the march, skirmishing, making an attack, and doubling through the fields and woods, 'o'er moor and fen, o'er crag and torrent" till — we capture the imaginary German front, then Mr. Editor, you would feel like saying, "send them right to Berlin, on after Kaiser Bill." As I said, we don't take those rumours seriously. We are content to know that when the time comes they will give us a chance to get a sprig from the moustache of the notorious Kaiser. So much for that subject.

Did you hear that we have a splendid reading room. We subscribe 3d. (6 cents) per month and in return are supplied with writing utensils, games and all the latest illustrated papers and magazines, including of course our own home papers. This recreation room was started by Lieut. Tait, and Corporal Jack Fox was unanimously elected President. We feel grateful to Lt.-Col. Burton for granting us permission to have this favour and our thanks are also due Lieut. Tait for his interest in the matter. It is a lovely place to spend an evening. I am writing this letter at one of the tables. On my left at another table, sits one of the most popular chaps in the regiment, Lance Corporal Jack Oakly, Jack is writing presumably to his best — and across the room our genial friend (everybody's friend) Pte. Stenlake is surrounded by an admiring group, as he gives an interesting account of the positions of the Allies, and his opinion as to where the next naval fight will take place. Good old Stenlake, we all love him, for he is one of the best that ever lived, he has just recovered from a cold, and we understand has been invited by the Methodist Congregation at Inverness to preach there on Sunday next. We congratulate him, for Inverness is a town of about 28,000 inhabitants, and we feel it an honour for one of our Newfoundland Boys to be invited there for such a purpose.

Inverness is just as popular as ever. Oh yes, some of us go there occasionally, and spend a very pleasant time. The people are more than kind, in fact we are sometimes tempted to overstay our passes and remain a few hours longer, but of course that would not do, so when the time is up, we reluctantly have to tear ourselves away and hire a conveyance to start for home. Any old conveyance will do, we are not particular,-automobiles, cabs, flying machines, or anything that can move. Inverness is only eleven miles from here, and our pass is up to 10 p.m. Well, those flying machines go at the rate of about 100 miles an hour, so we could easily leave there at five to ten and almost before we have time to change our mind, we are landed at Fort George. It is very exciting whizzing through the air at such an awful speed.

We are practising our shooting at present. (When I say we, I refer to B. Company — THE Company (ahem!) Capt. Alexander is O.C., our platoon is No. 8, in charge of Lieut. Nunns, Sergt. James is the Sergeant, and Lance Corporal Hoare is senior corporal. With such officers and N.C.O.'s we feel very proud of our platoon. Mr. Nunns is liked by all, and he takes great interest in the boys, who all try to do their best to make No. 8 right up to the mark. A few days ago a subscription was started amongst the men and a nice present given him, just to show our appreciation of his many kind acts. A concert is being held in Fort George Theatre tonight, many ladies and gentlemen from Inverness taking part, and judging by the last concert they held here we shall have something good.

Corporal Dick Sheppard has received another stripe and is now Sergt. Sheppard. Congratulations Dick, old boy, you are going ahead famously! In speaking of B. Company just now, I omitted to mention our Sergt.-Major (Mr. B. Dicks). Sergt.-Major Dicks is very popular amongst the men, who would do anything for him. Although he keeps us all up to the scratch, yet the orders are given in such pleasant terms that the men feel it a pleasure to obey. Last but by no means least, is Q.M. Strong. Charlie is another popular boy, and we are proud of him.

THIRD LETTER

—

Edinburgh Castle, Edinburgh,
Feb. 20th, 1915.

 E ARE NOW STATIONED AT EDINBURGH CASTLE. We left Fort George at 9:30 a.m., yesterday and were played to the station (Ardesier) by the Seaforths' band, they and the inhabitants gave us a grand send off and we think were sorry to lose us. As the train steamed out of the station the band played the old familiar "Should Auld Acquaintance."

The scenery is beautiful along the line, and we regret that owing to ours being a troop train we did not stop at any stations until we got to Perth. There we stayed about twenty minutes, and here we were again reminded of the goodness of the dear Scotch people (shall we ever forget!) for no sooner had the train stopped then waiters from the restaurant came forward with hot tea and sandwiches for every man, as much as one would be able to eat, all free of charge, presented us by the restaurant, and as we were about to leave Capt. Carty called for three cheers for Mr. Foster, Manager of the restaurant room.

These were given with a will, for we all did appreciate that nice hot tea.

At 6.30 we arrived at Edinburgh and it was here we had the reception, for the station was thronged with people all eager to catch a glimpse of the "Colonials," as we are often called. The band from the regiment at Edinburgh Castle was in waiting and played lots of patriotic airs, after which we started amidst cheering, from the thousands, who lined the streets all the way.

After arriving at the Castle we got our kit bags and blankets, assisted by the boys of the second Contingent, — amongst whom we met many old friends — then tea and turn in.

In the morning we had a chance to view the Castle, which is so interesting, built away back — so far back that is gives us a headache trying to trace the beginning. The Castle is on a rock, 443 feet above the sea level, and forms the most prominent feature of all the views of the City. No part of the present buildings, with the exception of the small Norman Chapel of Queen Margaret, dates further back than the fifteenth century. The Castle is entered by a drawbridge and through an archway, above which is the Guard-room. Further up is the Constables' Tower, now known as "Argyle Tower." Here the Earl of Argyle was imprisoned previous to his execution. Still further up by Fogg's Gate, is one of the most interesting objects of the Castle. It is the Chapel of Queen Margaret, who died in 1093. On the east side of the Square are the ancient Royal apartments, "Crown Room." In a room on the ground floor, Mary Queen of Scots gave birth to James VI, on June 19th, 1566, and on the South is the Banquetting Hall. This Hall, the "Magna Curia" or great Hall of the Castle, is referred to in the Exchequer Rolls as having been erected in 1434, and since restored, and the Hall is filled with ancient arms and armour and other relics, dating back to the fifteenthth century. In one place we found a demi-suit of black armour worn by a footman in time of James VI, (about 1570); in another place, a long swivel gun with flint lock, date on lock 1793, and again here is a suit of bright steel armour worn in the time of Cromwell, old time pistols, flint locks and so on. The Hall is filled with ancient curios, a sight indeed worth seeing, helmets and armour worn at the battle of Bannockburn. You can imagine how we felt as we gazed on those relics of ancient days. In the Crown Room we saw the crown first worn by Bruce, and last by Charles II, in 1651. It was lost in 1707 and found in this very room 100 years later through Sir Walter Scott. Here also are the sword of James IV, Jewel of Garter, James VI., Coronation Ring, Charles I, and many other valuable jewels used by old time Scottish sovereigns. The next room to this is the bedroom of Queen Mary.

After seeing this we wandered outside again, but there are so many things to see I wish I had time to tell you all. Looking on those old relics makes a fellow think and feel like being good — for a little while at any rate. I forgot to mention the Forth Bridge which we passed over before entering Edinburgh. This is the longest bridge in the world, about 2 1/2 miles long. It took seven years to build. We are seeing things to remember for a lifetime.

All the boys are well and happy, and who wouldn't be happy under the circumstances? Why here we are, the 750 of us, the guard over this wonderful Castle (for the Scotch regiment left on our arrival). We are — in a way — monarchs of all we survey. Isn't it a great honour for us Newfoundland boys to be in charge of this grand old place? What we shall have to tell you all when we get back, and please God, we hope to all return again.

FOURTH LETTER

—

Stob's Camp, Scotland,

May 20th, 1915.

 E ARE NOW AT STOB'S CAMP about fifty-three miles from Edinburgh, with about 20,000 inhabitants, and famous for its tweeds.

This is a second edition of Salisbury Plains — with the exception of the mud — and talking about mud, we have very little here, and we are not a bit sorry, would you believe it? Our Camp is laid out in a beautiful spot and the boys make a great showing, it is worth seeing, when we all get on parade, 1,300 strong, and — as the Edinburgh people said — the fittest looking body of men they ever saw. Just on our left is a regiment of the A.S.C., (Army Service Corps). Our boys often play them in football and other games, and it goes without saying the Newfoundlanders generally come off best. On our right is a detention camp containing 10,000 german prisoners (spell German with a small g please, they don't deserve a capital letter). The air is grand, and by the time we leave here this will be a body of men "hard as nails", for we are hard at drill from 5:30 a.m. until 4:30 p.m., skirmishing, squad-drill, company drill and physical exercise, and with regard to the physical drill, we have a drill instructor, an old Seaforth man — and what he doesn't know about it, is not worth talking about, he is a whole team in himself. In addition to this he has organized boxing and wrestling matches for the evenings, which are very interesting. Corporal Stan Goodyear is high liner so far, and Stan is a hard man to beat, for he has a grip like iron and a punch like the fall of a thunderbolt.

The skirmishes here are very interesting as there are some nice hills to climb and rivers to cross, but we don't need pontoons for the rivers, as the water is not very deep.

Several changes have been made in the officers commanding companies. Capt. Carty is still O.C. of A. Company, and Capt. Alexander of B. Company. Capt. Bernard is now in charge of C. Company, Capt. March of D. Company, Capt. O'Brien has charge of E. Company, and all take a great interest in the men. Of course each Company look on their commander as THE BEST, and quite naturally we of B. Company think there is nobody on earth like Capt. Alexander, he is indeed very popular and considerate, and there is not a man in B. Company who would not die for him. Now I must "blow" again, (as I did in my last letter), I must say a word about our platoon — THE platoon — Lieut. Bain is in charge since Lieut. Nunns left, and he is liked well by all the men, nothing seems too much trouble for him to do for No. 8 platoon, and the boys are ready to swear by him at any time.

Our tent is No. 21, and we have quite a nice crowd, W. Harnett, T. Mouland, F. Keel, A. Purchase, A. Newman, A.M.

TOP ROW - Left to Right. - Arch Newman, Thomas Mouland, Noel Gilbert, Walter Haines, Walter Kearley, Arthur Purchase.

BOTTOM ROW. - Robert Haley, Fred Keel, Arthur Pratt, Frank Lind, Wilfred Harvey

Pratt, R. Haley, W. Harvey, W. Kearley, N. Gilbert, E. White, and myself — just a dozen. We have lots of music, accordion, tin whistle, mouth organ, gramophone, and as soon as we get room will put in a small organ. Oh yes, the boys are intent on having the organ, even if we have to move the washstand and dinner table out to make room for it, and then we can enjoy the evenings in fine style for we have some nice singers amongst us.

We are so thankful to the kind friends at home for all they are doing for us. The action of the Government in allowing our mail to pass free of charge is very much appreciated by us all, and the kind ladies who are doing so much in the way of sending clothing and luxuries, we shall never forget them. The hardest problem we (smokers) have to face is the tobacco, it is almost impossible to get good tobacco in this country, a stick of "Mayo" is indeed a luxury.

It is rumoured we leave here in a couple of weeks for Bedford, but one cannot say, as there are so many stories. We hear a different one every day, but wherever we go the First Newfoundland Regiment will do their part.

This is one of the finest days we've had since landing on this side, and a nice day in Scotland is beyond description, it makes a fellow feel that life is worth living. I am writing this sitting on the grass outside our tent and the sun is simply pouring down. We have just come back from a skirmish over the hills and this rest is good, the boys are enjoying themselves at various games, just behind me some of them are kicking a football and a few minutes ago the ball came down and landed with a bump at my feet. I thought it was a bomb and the Germans had come at last, and was just going to run for my arms, only to find it was the poor innocent ball kicked out of bounds by some reckless player. Lots of the boys have gone to Hawick, "that sensational town of Hawick." It is said that the *Hawick Daily Times* published an item yesterday with great headlines, saying that "two horses were seen in the street at one time," — wonderful — but I give this for what it is worth, probably there is no truth in the story, forgive me for the joke, but we chaps after Edinburgh, don't look on any place now, probably that is it, and let me say, I don't think any of us will ever forget our visit to Edinburgh and the wonderful sights seen there — space forbids me talk of it now. Some day, please God, we shall be able to tell you all about that lovely city, and its people, the kindness shown us, and about that wonderful Castle (Edinburgh Castle). One would never tire going over it and seeing the old relics of different ages. We may not appreciate it now the same as we will some day, after we've "been to Berlin" and back to old Terra Nova, then we will indeed realize what an honour has been shown us. We shall have so much to talk about.

All the boys are well and happy, and everything goes along merrily.

FIFTH LETTER.

—

Stob's Camp,
Via Hawick, Scotland,
May 26th, 1915.

 THOUGHT I'D DROP A LINE ABOUT EMPIRE DAY (24th May). We had a general holiday — all excepting the mess-orderlies and unfortunately I was Mess Orderly that day, but I managed to steal away (don't tell) for a few minutes in the afternoon. The tug-of-war was very interesting, won by A Company which had put up an excellent team. The programme was made up of football fives, mile races, sack races, boxing matches, etc., and everybody enjoyed themselves. It was like the day of the races down at Quidi Vidi with of course, the pond and race boats left out. We had everything else, in fact we over did the Nfld. Regatta, for we had this more on the style of a circus; two negro boxers appeared on the field and entertained the audience between each item of the programme. We forgot we were 53 1/4 miles from Edinburgh and 2 1/2 miles from Hawick (oh, I mustn't forget Hawick) and imagined ourselves down by the side of Quidi Vidi once more. Lots of visitors from town came to see the sports, and also many of the A.S.C. (Army Service Corps) and A. and S.H.

(Argyle and Sutherland Highlanders) who are camped near us. The officers took great interest in the games and when such men as Capts. Carty, Bernard, Lieuts. Ayre, Rowsell, Raley and others take hold it goes without saying that the affair will be a success. Lt.-Col. De Burton also took great interest in the Regatta.

All the boys are well and enjoyed themselves. The new Y.M.C.A. opened a day or two ago and we find this very convenient for there we can go in any day and sit down, write letters (all stationary provided free) or read, and for a penny (2¢) one can get a cup of hot coffee or cocoa, for another penny you can buy a cake or bun, just imagine "a meal for 4¢." "Going some" you will say. We can also get this cup of cocoa and cake in the canteens for the same price. It is very nice for us especially on an evening before retiring to be able to have a nice hot drink and a cake, and our only remark as we wander out is "Oh if they only kept Mayo's tobacco for sale," instead of the horrible weed we have to torture ourselves with.

Lance-Corpl. Nugent was lately promoted to Corporal. We must congratulate him, the promotion is well deserved. Mr. Nugent is in charge of the pioneer work and not a better man in the Regiment could be found for this job. He and his squad kept the camp in perfect order and goodness help any person found throwing rubbish about, for Corporal Nugent in indeed "an enemy of dirt."

I paid another visit to Hawick last evening and in passing down one of the streets two ladies looked at the badges on our shoulders and one said Neld (they took the F. for an E.) where is Neld?" I said it is not Neld it is Nfld. — Newfoundland! "Oh," she said, "that's in Canada, isn't it?" I looked around for a brick. Canada again! "No," I roared, "Newfoundland is a separate Colony. Do they teach geography in your schools here?" and we hurried on in disgust. How hard it is to teach the people that Nfld. and Canada are two separate colonies, but we'll teach them in Hawick yet, same as we did in Nairn, Inverness and Edinburgh, supposing we have to parade the streets and sing Mr. James Murphy's songs and keep them awake at night, for those songs have the real Newfoundland touch about them.

SIXTH LETTER.

Stob's Camp,
Near Hawick, Scotland,
June 4, 1915.

E ARE STILL AT STOB'S CAMP; and have no idea when we move. This is a splendid camping ground.

The District General paid us a visit yesterday and the whole battalion turned out in full marching order, everybody alert and everything polished as bright as new shillings. We then went skirmishing for about eight miles across the plains. The general and staff meanwhile took up a position on the highest hill and watched us through their glasses. Our object was to capture an old farmhouse that is A. B. D. and E. Company's, while C. Company, "held the fort." We were to drive C. Company from their position and take the farm, which we eventually did without the loss of many men and horses. Thereafter we returned to camp, and, it being the King's birthday, the bill of fare for dinner was something extra. First soup, then roast beef, potatoes, turnips, etc., followed by pudding, fruit and tea, then "God save the King" was enthusiastically sung, Wilfred Harvey leading off with the cornet and Fred Keel with the accordion.

We are sorry to lose Corporal Eddie Hoare, he having left B. Company and taken a position in the transport department; "Eddie" is a popular chap and everybody regrets his transfer to the transports, where no doubt he will find greater scope for his talent, for if there is one thing Eddie is all at home at, it is in handling horses. To see him tearing across the green sometimes standing upon the horse's back, with the reins in his teeth, reminds me of the times I've seen the circus going through Canada. Good luck Eddie! Whilst wishing you no harm, No. 4 platoon hopes soon to see you back with them again.

Wilfred Harvey has been transferred to the orderly room as stenographer and general assistant. Wilfred is a nice boy and one of the number in our tent. George Butler (formerly of the Royal Stores tailoring department), is still busy sewing on buttons and doing general tailoring for the boys. It goes without saying George is just the boy can do it.

We wonder what sort of weather you are having in Newfoundland, here it is just perfect, so warm all the time. There is a lake just a short distance away in which we often bathe.

On June 10th Lady MacGregor is going to make the presentation of new colours, for the Newfoundland Regiment, this will be a gala day for us. Everybody will turn out with buttons and brasses shining that day. We are practising the march past every other day for this event.

The Y.M.C.A. is doing a rushing business every day. They provide stationery free of charge, tables at which to sit and write, books to read and a piano. Last, but not least, serving behind the counters are some dozen Scottish lassies, who do all in their power to make things go pleasantly, ever ready to see that the soldiers are promptly served with coffee, cakes, sandwiches and soft drinks.

Stob's Camp,

Near Hawick, Scotland,

June 17, 1915.

TILL AT STOB'S, although most of us expected to have been moved before this. The weather is beautiful; it makes us wonder do they have any winter in this country.

We are hard at work every day, chiefly bayonet practice. Let me tell you a little about our bayonet fighting. No doubt it will be interesting to a good many of your readers. We have as Instructor an old soldier, Sergt. Major Somebody, who knows all about gymnastics from the word "go," in fact we sometimes think he is "on wires," for you never saw anybody who could put himself into such shapes as old "Gym", as he is familiarly known amongst the boys. Well, they have Hessian sacks filled with straw hung about four feet from the ground, an obstacle about three feet high in front, and further in front is a trench — a regular trench as at the Front. We have to rush out "in fours" with fixed bayonets, "kill the Germans" in the trench, and hop over the obstacles on to the sacks, which represent so many more of the enemy. We "kill them" with a vicious lunge, and rush forward, jump over a deep hole filled with water (six feet deep, ten feet wide), and you just bet we do jump, for the man who misses simply goes into the water to the amusement of the boys. I can assure you we all try to jump the ditch for it is much more comfortable being dry than wet. We then "slope arms" and return, and the next four go forward. We are all well acquainted with trench digging now. You bet it gives us a great idea of what real war is. You ought to see those bags of straw after we're done with them, simply perforated from top to bottom. I hope you won't think us bloodthirsty, but we often regret it is not Germans who are there instead of sacks. Wouldn't the boys just "paste 'em."

We had a very interesting time on the 10th, the presentation of Colours. Quite a lot of people were in from town to see it. Lady MacGregor made the presentation, and Lieut. J. Fox was the officer in charge of the Colour Party. The Flag was handed to Lady MacGregor by Capt. Carty. She made a graceful speech and passed the Flag to Mr. Fox, who received it kneeling on one knee. Clergymen of all denominations took part in the service, which opened by the singing of "Brightly gleams our Banner." At the presentation we presented arms and it was a fine sight. Speeches were made by Sir William MacGregor and the General in Command (Scotland), who said he was proud to be able to say that this fine body of men were trained in Scotland. (We wondered what about Pleasantville and the South Side Hills and the *Florizel* — but enough said). Our Colonel also made a speech, thanking Sir Wm. and Lady MacGregor. Then came the march past, wish you could have seen that, but the moving picture man was there all the time. At the close we sang "God Save the King," our band struck up and we returned to camp, everybody happy. The next night we went to the picture palace at Hawick, and beheld the same thing over again on the screen. It looked good, the boys marching in splendid order. They certainly can do things in Scotland. Just imagine seeing ourselves in the "movies" a day after the picture was taken, and the cameras were there also. Now we can buy postcard views of the whole thing. Surely we have some reason to swell out our chests and look important. I hope some of the St. John's picture houses will get the film for it is worth seeing, and the chaps can be readily recognized.

All the boys are well, and why not, in this health-giving place. We will be all sunburned brown by the time of leaving.

We have to do guard all around the camp, at the store houses and railway. I was on at the railway last night, but it was very quiet, not a German or Austrian or Turk or "any old nationality" put in an appearance, not even a zeppelin to break the monotony (probably they knew 'I' was on guard). Still we have to watch all these places, for one cannot tell what will happen.

Yesterday was bathing day (we have bathing parades once a week). There is a lovely pond just a short distance off, and it is very exciting. There are some splendid swimmers in our lot. Arthur Jackman, Pat Walsh, Sam Cole, Harris Oake, and others. They can do anything in the water. Our Colonel was present. He always takes a great interest in healthy exercise, and if we don't prove 'fit' it will not be his fault. Just as we got out of the water a Company of A. and S. Highlanders came along for a bathe, but they cannot "hold a candle" to our boys when it comes to swimming.

On Saturday I got leave and paid a visit to Edinburgh. If Edinburgh was beautiful before, it is much more so now, the flowers all in bloom and the look of summer everywhere. I noticed that since we left they have put women conductors on the cars, so that the men can go to the Front. Same in Glasgow. (Now, who said women should not have the vote?) God bless the women. You ought to see them in the streets trying to urge young men to join the colours and wishing they were men so that they could go. I heard of lots of the lassies in Edinburgh who broke engagements with their sweethearts because they would not join the Army. I won't say that some of those lassies took up with Newfoundlanders instead. Oh, no, I won't say that, it's not right to tell tales out of school. Oh, the women are patriotic in this country. If a young man (a civilian) is looking for a girl the first question he is asked by the lady is "Why don't you enlist, then come back and I'll talk to you, for I could never marry a coward?" I took a run on the cars in Edinburgh (not because there were lady conductors) and found as usual every courtesy and half price to soldiers. The price is two pence (4¢) go where you like, but they only charge us one penny. Then as soon as we get on the Leith line the charge for soldiers is nothing, they are even more generous than the Edinburgh Company, for a soldier can stay in a Leith car and go as far as he likes free. At the Waverley Station we were asked into a restaurant and given a lunch, cocoa, biscuits, etc., all free to soldiers (civilians charged regular price). I thought I was in fairy land. As long as you have the King's uniform on, the people go out of their way to oblige you, but the poor civilians have a hard time of it.

There is a clock in Prince's St. Gardens made entirely of "flowers" the diameter of the clock is about ten feet and it gives the correct time. The hands of course are flowers in bloom, and it is worth while seeing them move. At first glance it appears like a bed of flowers, but as one draws nearer we see what they represent, and many visit the gardens especially to see this wonderful clock.

On Sunday, 6th inst., the evening service at the Baptist Church, Hawick, was conducted by Private Stenlake (formerly Rev. W.K. Stenlake, Twillingate District), assisted by Lewis Head and Lance-Corpl. Taylor. Wherever Stenlake goes the people soon discover what a jolly good sort he is (I hope this term is not out of place to use towards a parson, but if it is I am sure Stenlake will forgive his brother soldier this time). Mr. Stenlake has made himself very popular both in the Regiment and amongst the people of the different places we visit. Amongst the boys of the First Newfoundland Regiment, Stenlake is thought a great deal of. He is always good hearted and pleasant, always ready with a cheery word or smile for anybody with whom he comes in contact, and amongst the people it is just the same, for we had scarcely landed in Stob's when he was asked to preach in the Baptist Church at Hawick, and on Sunday, the sixth, a large congregation was present, all eager to hear this talented young man. A lot of the boys from the Regiment also attended. Mr. Stenlake gave an excellent sermon, taking his text from the Epistle of Paul the Apostle to the Romans, First Chap., Sixteenth verse: "For I am not ashamed of the Gospel of Christ," and all present were much interested in the excellent and thoughtful discourse. Well, done, Stenlake, you are bringing honour to the Nfld. Regt. Privates Clarrage and Pickett sang "Some day the silver cords will break."

Rev. Mr. Clark, a native of this part, has been appointed Chaplain to the First Newfoundland Regiment. It is strange that no native of Terra Nova could be found for this position. I am sure there are several of our clergymen at home who would be only too pleased to accept the post, or what about Stenlake? He knows all the boys and their different ways, and can get around and talk to them. No more popular appointment could be made than by placing dear old Stenlake as Chaplain for we all adore him.

Private Noel Gilbert of B. Company, has received a commission as 2nd Lieut. in the Royal Welsh Fusiliers. Gilbert was one of the number in our tent, and we were sorry to lose him. The night before leaving, Gilbert, in his usual open-hearted way, treated all the boys in splendid style, chocolates, fruits, cigars, and cigarettes, lemonade and ice cream. The celebration was kept up until lights out, and ended with singing "For he's a jolly good fellow." In the morning we gave him a good send off as he left for Hawick to entrain. Many were the wishes of good luck and prosperity he received as Gilbert is an excellent chap, one of the best in the world, and the whole Company are sorry to lose him. I know we shall hear of him again, and wherever he may be he will make his mark.

Stob's Camp,

July 14th, 1915.

HERE IS ANOTHER RUMOUR that we will be moving shortly, but where to? — and how this latest story gets abroad is that a day or two ago, the General Officer commanding this district inspected us again, this time accompanied by two Lord Provosts. One, the Lord Provost of Selkirk, in the course of his speech said he wished us every good luck when we go South. The boys think he meant somewhere in Scotland. These gentlemen gave us great speeches and didn't they praise up this splendid regiment — no swank — (that's Scotch). If all they say about us is correct then we will carry all before us, beat the Germans to a standstill, enter Berlin with a flourish return to Newfoundland — most of us — and live happily ever afterwards, and go to — yes to heaven when we die. But to be serious, they spoke in splendid terms of the Newfoundland Regiment, said we were a fine looking body of men, and would indeed do our share in the task before us. We were the fittest looking lot of men they had seen in this great war. I wish the Governor, Sir Walter Davidson and Sir Edward

Morris could have heard these speeches, it would have made them feel that their efforts in raising this regiment was indeed appreciated by the Government and people on this side.

We are all so thankful to the dear friends in Terra Nova for the Mayo-Linds' (they arrived Saturday), and how much we appreciate all you have done for us. The efforts of the *Daily News* we will never forget. Little did I think that the few words in one of my letters would result in such a generous donation of tobacco, but that "a stick of Mayo is a luxury," is certainly true, it is the tobacco we all enjoy. This lot will likely be distributed in a day or two, and if anybody doubts our love for Mayos then they ought to be present on the day it is given out. God bless the dear friends at home for coming forward like this, you may be sure we shall never forget them. It is needless to say I am now called "Mayo" Lind.

F. Company arrived a few days ago and are quite settled now. Camp life is rather hard at first, but after a little while it comes as natural as anything, and soon this new Company will be as happy as we are. We met many old friends amongst the lot, including Boyd Crocker and Frank Burke, and they all told us of the glorious trip across, the visit to Gibraltar and the splendid way they were treated on the *Calgarian*. Then I suddenly thought of our passage across on the *Florizel* — but we are just going to forget all about that trip. Lieut. Nunns came over in charge of the new company. We gave him a great welcome, and hope he will remain with us for Mr. Nunns is the idol of No. 8 Platoon, and we were almost thinking he had gone back on the boys of B. Company, but no, he returns with the same old genial smile for all. F. Company are camped next to E., it is a pretty sight to see the tents all arranged so nicely, first the officers', then in rotation A. B. C. D. E. and F. Companies. I wonder where we shall be when it reaches X. Y. Z. but hope Germany will be wiped off the map long before then.

I am writing in the Y.M.C.A. Just at present it is pretty well crowded, somebody is playing 'Who Stole my Kit Bag?' and at the table near me Pte. Walter Murphy is writing a letter to the Belgian lassie he met in Newcastle. Walter is a splendid chap and has just returned from a visit to Newcastle and tells us what a nice time he had, meeting such a reception on all sides. There are lots of Belgian refugees there and Walter (this is a secret) fell in love with one of the Belgians. He expects to take another trip there soon — of course. Well done, Walter, but we hope that you won't get so far gone as to forget Terra Nova.

Very early Sunday morning we had quite an exciting time in our tent, another visit from some of the numerous sheep about here. The poor innocent creatures, about six of them, not knowing where they were wandering came through our lines and up to the tent occupied by us. After knocking down our clothes line, and tipping over a bucket of strawberries, which Bob Haley and Arch Newman had picked that evening, they entered the doorway (I mean opening), and, before discovered, had kicked over our sideboard (pineapple box we use to keep bread in) and broken three bottles of pickles and two dozen eggs, then lastly, but not least, they tried to climb over the organ which came down with a crash and we awoke. Then the fun began, Bob Haley took the first thing at hand to throw (we discovered after that it was a bun of bread), and what a scamper we had to clear them out. However, we soon put the run on them, for as a last resource Wilfred Harvey blew a blast on the bugle which put them to flight.

NINTH LETTER.

Stob's Camp,

July 20th, 1915.

E ARE STILL AT STOB'S. One of our chaps had a dream last night, and he dreamt that it was 1920, five years hence — the war was over. He was in London and somewhere heard the King say to Kitchener, "Well, Kitchener, the war is over and we have won. Our armies did remarkably well, but how did that Newfoundland Regiment get on?" "Oh, by Jove, your Majesty," said Kitchener, "that reminds me, they must be still at Stob's."

The Mayo's tobacco was distributed on Friday. Some people say that Friday is an unlucky day, but you cannot make the Newfoundland Regiment believe that now. There was joy in every smoker's breast that day, for you know what a good smoke is to us chaps, and we certainly all of us greatly appreciate this gift of Mayo-Linds from the home-folk.

B. Purchase (brother of Pte. Arthur Purchase, B. Company,) paid us a visit Saturday. He is now on H.M.S. *Eclipse*, but was on Admiral Beatty's ship during the action in which the *Blucher* was destroyed. Purchase has a wound in his leg, (now quite well) which he received from a piece of shrapnel fired from the *Blucher* in her death agonies. You see, Newfoundlanders seem to be doing their bit all the time.

I was going to say something about the war, but looking over the *Daily News*, mail after mail, I see you get more war news than we do here — you see we are still at Stob's. It is said that Turkey is about to withdraw from the fight. I expect they are simply fed up with those 'headaches' from H.M.S. *Queen Elizabeth*.

Our new Major has arrived, and yesterday there was another route march, about fifteen miles. On the way back, we had a bit of excitement coming across the fields. The rabbits are very plentiful, and we were marching at ease then. Well it was great fun to see the rabbits running in all directions. The boys killed about twenty and of course several of the tents had rabbit suppers last night. We have route marches four and five times a week.

You will be pleased to know that Corpl. Nugent, who has charge of the pioneers, has been promoted to Sergeant. This is a well earned promotion, for Sergeant Nugent is the right man in the right place. No doubt nearly everybody in St. John's knows former Constable Green. Well, he is now in charge of the Regimental Police, and has risen to the rank of Sergeant. Sergt. Green is another good man, and does his duty holding the respect of all; at the same time he is liked by everybody. Congratulations to both, also to W. Ryan, M. Knight, and W. Hutchings who have been made full Corporals, the three of them jolly good fellows.

We often meet the German prisoners. When on parade we come across them in droves (the word aptly applies to cattle) under charge of guards, and what a miscellaneous lot they are! Some are in sailor uniform, and we read the names on their caps and note "Blucher" "Dresden," etc.; some are in soldier's uniforms, and wear a kind of blue-grey. There are civilians of all classes, some apparently in good positions, others by their looks taken from the slums of the great cities of this country but all united — against their will — and with picks and shovels working on the roads. Some of the K.O.S.B.'s (Kings Own Scottish Borderers) and Royal Scots are camped on the right of us. One can't help noticing the distinction made between officers and men as compared with the Canadian and Newfoundland Regiment. A few days ago one of the K.O.S.B.'s privates reported sick to his Corporal, who happened to be a new chap just from London. When asked what the trouble was, the private said, "A pain in my abdomen." "Only officers have abdomens," shouted the Corporal.

You ought to hear our band now. They have got on to all the latest tunes, and it is worth hearing when we are on the march. Stan Tuck, an old Millertown friend, is one of the buglers. Stan is one of the youngest boys in the regiment, and one of the pluckiest also.

The Salvation Army from Hawick (Hawick, oh yes, they have a Salvation Army there) pay us a visit now and again. They come inside our lines and favour us with lots of nice singing, and generally go away with a nice collection.

They say we are going to Bedford shortly, don't know how

true. Some of our boys, in fact most of us, will not be sorry to move from Stob's and doubtless from Bedford we will go on to the front, "somewhere in France," or to the Dardanelles, but, Germans or Turks, the Newfoundland Regiment will make them remember our visit. Our stay at Edinburgh will never be forgotten. The people there are not done talking about us yet, they claim we are the fittest looking lot of men every stationed there, so you can just draw your own conclusions as to what we will do with the enemy.

Former Corporal Gerald Byrne is now Sergeant. Gerald is one of the most popular men in the Regiment, and we are glad to see him go ahead.

P.S. — "Mayo's is always good."

TENTH LETTER.

—————

Stob's Camp,

July 29th, 1915.

HIS, I TRUST, IS THE LAST LETTER you will receive from me at Stob's Camp for we understand that the Battalion (A. B. C. and D. Company's) move in a day or two to Aldershot for our final "polish" before going to the front. E. and F. Company's are not going with us but move to Ayr, Scotland; 150 men from E. Company have been transferred to the first four Company's to make a full battalion — we trust the men from E. Company fully realize the honour conferred upon them. There have been so many tales of us going to one place and another that we hardly know what to believe, but this we think is correct. All will be sorry to leave Bonnie Scotland "where the heather and the bluebells grow." Our stay in Scotland has indeed been pleasant and the great kindness shown us by the people everywhere will live in our memory forever. Don't know how long we will be in Aldershot, expect only a few days before we move to the front and there face the grim reality of war, this war, the greatest in history, and may we all do our bit towards keeping the old flag flying!

Rev. J. Bell (formerly of the Cathedral, St. John's) paid us a visit last week and was shown through the camp by Sergt. Major B. Dicks. The Reverend gentleman takes a great interest in Newfoundlanders, he visited us at Salisbury Plains, Fort George and Edinburgh Castle and now here. We were all glad to see him, he had a cheery word for everyone.

I paid a visit to Hawick on Sunday (Hawick is not so bad at all — the more we see of it the better we like it). The town is full of men in khaki belonging to different regiments stationed in Hawick or its surroundings, and there are some nice families, they are proud of Hawick — Hawick-among-the-Hills is the name the inhabitants love so well — with its public buildings, pleasure-parks, well-kept streets, handsome villa residences and its pleasant environment. The name Hawick is traced to Hagawic or fenced-habitation and the first historic mention of it is found in connection with the evangel-istic labours of St. Cuthbert who established an early Christian Sanctuary there. The first church we see on entering the town is St. Cuthbert's (C. of E.) At Haggisha or Burnflat close to the Vertish Hall overlooking the town, Robt. Paterson was born in 1716. We bid good bye to Hawick-among-the-Hills in a day or two and perhaps some of us in the future may visit there again.

I was talking to a Royal Scot soldier just from the front, wounded. These Scotch are gritty chaps, this one is just aching to get back to the firing line, and he tells some awful things in connection with those devilish Germans. They seem to have made up their minds to win this campaign no matter what they resort to, but they will soon realize that their day is done. This soldier spoke of the poison gas the Germans use, Chlorine, a dark greenish-yellow gas — the name Chlorine is derived from the Greek word meaning green. From the same word is derived the medical term Chlorosis for what used to be called "green-sickness" (Shakespeare uses the word in Romeo and Juliet) or anaemia. The pallor of the disease gave a greenish tint to the face. To get a little idea of what the gas is like which our soldiers face you have only to think of chloride of lime, but the gas chlorine used by the Germans is very much stronger and has the power of decomposing and destroying the mucus membrane lining of the nose and lungs. An accident liberating even a small quantity of chlorine will give workers in a laboratory all the symptoms of a severe cold, and the agonies suffered by the victims of German deceit and unfair war methods are those of bronchitis, multiplied many times over. This chap says he has been fortunate enough to escape the gas thus far but has seen victims several times. But the Kaiser, and his savages, will pay for it some day, for surely the great and good God will never allow a nation to exist that uses such horrible means as these Germans do. We pity them when the day of reckoning comes.

Sergt. J. Robinson is still in charge of the Officers' Mess and it goes without saying that John is the right man for the position. He is ably assisted by Peter Mansfield — the genial Peter who always has a pleasant smile for everyone. Peter is very popular and we have no record of him ever having been seen with a cross or unpleasant look, he has a good word for everyone and everyone has a good word for Peter. Former Quarter Master Sergt. Strong of B. Company has been promoted, and is now Sergt. Major of F. Company Charlie is one of the best that ever lived. Private A.M. Pratt of B. Company has just returned from a trip to Edinburgh. Arthur is a genial fellow, and before he enlisted, was well and favourably known throughout the country as representative of the Direct Agencies, Ltd.

Since writing the above I find that the orders are posted saying we leave for Aldershot on Monday August second. When we get there I hope to be able to send you a few interesting notes.

ELEVENTH LETTER.

———

Aldershot,

August 8th, 1915.

 EFORE THIS you have, no doubt, heard that the Regiment has moved to this famous camping ground, having arrived here on Tuesday morning. When leaving Stob's camp the people came from all places nearby to witness our departure and Hawick was well represented at the station, to wish us God-speed. Dear old Scotland we are all sorry to leave, for from the time we went there until leaving there was nothing but kindness shown and we shall never forget the sons and daughters of the Heather.

All have heard of Aldershot, for its fame is world-wide. It is the First Army Corps district and its commander is always a soldier of great distinction, one who has served well his country. The present Commander-in-Chief is Sir Archibald Hunter, who has nearly all the letters of the alphabet after his name, having distinguished himself in the Soudan, commanded a division in South Africa, afterward was Governor of Gibraltar and is now head of this great place and of course our Commander-in-Chief also. We occupy Badajos Barracks on

the Wellington Line and nothing could be more comfortable.
What a change from the camp; for here we have every convenience, the rooms are large, containing twenty-eight men and a
sergeant in charge. Sergt. James is in charge of our room, and it
goes without saying everything is spick and span in No. 17. He
is ably assisted by Corpl. Fred. Mercer and Lance-Corpl. Chas.
Hammond. There are large dining rooms on the next flat and
two platoons eat in each room. Corpl. O. Vaughan, Pat.
Walsh, C. Hammond and J. Caul attend to the wants of the
men in 7 and 8 platoons and all goes merrily.

Aldershot has become the centre of many military devel-
opments, amongst others the making of airships. Important
work in the training of the soldiers is carried on at the great
gymnasiums and provision has been made for social well-be-
ing, for there are numerous recreation rooms and soldier's
institutes, where we may go and play billiards, play other
games, write letters (material provided free) or we may borrow
a book of almost any kind. Nothing is left undone for the
soldiers' welfare. The town about us is quite up to date, a man
can buy anything from a uniform button to a horse and cab.
Wellington Avenue, where our barracks are situated, contains
the statue of the famous Duke of Wellington erected at Hyde
Park in 1846 and afterwards removed to its present site.
Caesar's camp in the neighbourhood is very ancient. It is said
that Alfred the Great fortified himself there 1,100 years ago
and Roman coins have been found, various emperors being
represented thereon such as Diocletian, Constatine, Alexander,
Severus and Domitian.

Yesterday we had a sham-battle each man having five rounds of ammunition. It was great. We skirmished across the plains outside for five or six miles and finally attacked and captured the position held by the enemy. Sir Archibald Hunter reviewed us on Friday and we had a great time on that day. Everybody turned out and our band in charge of Corporal Jack Oakley, played its best.

Sunday morning we attended church parade at the different military churches. It was a grand sight, so many soldiers from the numerous regiments; there are about 250,000 soldiers about here. Everything is military, strictly so, even to the ushers in the Church; they stood in the door, and as we approached the entrance and looked in, I saw several of them looking so fierce with moustaches waxed to a pin point, not a word out of them, but signalling with their arms, to place the different battalions in their positions. I said to myself "Are we going in church or slipping off to the front?" No smiles of welcome from those hard visages, no "Glad to see you, do come again next Sunday, and we are having a special meeting on Wednesday evening, come, we shall expect you." No, nothing of that sort, it was simply business, big business. How dare you smile! I shudder when I look forward to next Sunday. I hope the Colonel will arrange to have service in the barracks, I would as soon face the Germans as these ushers, but enough of this.

Wednesday evening a couple of us went down town, and passing a church, (Wesley Church) we went in, and beheld our friend Stenlake again on the platform. Mr. Stenlake preached a beautiful sermon from the text, "Go ye into all the world and preach the Gospel." Just imagine, we arrived on Tuesday, and Wednesday night they have discovered our talented comrade. It is always the same wherever we go. I shall not be a bit surprised when we are at the front if some day Stenlake is missing to find him in a German trench preaching to the Germans, for everybody seems to discover him.

The last regiment which occupied our barracks was the Devonshire, they are now at the front. This is indeed a wonderful place, and if we stand at the window facing the road, we see a continuous stream of soldiers, horse and foot, passing forth and back. There is no stop; like Tennyson's brook they seem to go on for ever.

London is 34¼ miles from here, fare to soldiers two shillings and sixpence for return ticket. Reading is nineteen miles away. Farnburgh, where the airships are kept, is 2¼ miles, and Farnham three miles. All those places I hope to see shortly.

It seems like old times to see the flying machines flitting about. Viewed in the distance they look like giant horse-stingers, the comparison is ridiculous. None of us have had a ride to London on one yet, that is a pleasure in store — we hope.

Although moving to such a lovely spot, yet we regret the move has taken away some of our good friends. A. and B. Companies are now on one side of the barracks, and C. and D. on the other. At Stob's the tent next ours was one of C. and contained a genial crowd — good neighbours — Nix Hunt, Stan Harvey and others, and many a pleasant joke was passed. Now they are separated from us.

TWELFTH LETTER.

———

Aldershot,

August 13, 1915.

 ESTERDAY — MEMORABLE DAY — Lord Kitchener came from London and inspected the battalion. There were about 20,000 men present from different regiments besides ours, but the Newfoundland Regiment was the only one Kitchener addressed. There is nothing put on about this great warrior, just plain outspoken straight-from-the-shoulder talk, and almost his first words were: "I am sending you to the Dardanelles shortly, so be prepared, for when the order comes it will come sharply," and as far as we can learn since then, I find that we will be away *within two weeks*, so probably by the time this letter is in print, the Newfoundland regiment will have left the shores of England to face the foe. May we do our part and bring honour to Terra Nova; it will not be all fun, for my opinion is we have had the best of it so far, and now comes the sterner side. I shall try and drop you a line from time to time when we get along, and shall hope to be able to give a good account of how things are going in the Dardanelles. F. Company and part of E. Company are, as you

49

know, moving to Ayr, Scotland, that is to be our depot. We all were glad to hear we will be moving shortly, for we have been here on this side ten months.

Today the Colonel called A. and B. Companies out, and asked who would like to sign on for the duration of the war as our year is up shortly, and I can tell you the Newfoundlanders soon showed the stuff they are made of, for all with a few exceptions, signed on. We then had to parade to the Doctor and undergo another examination, and as far as I can learn, everybody passed; why not? for if a fellow was "fit" twelve months ago he ought to be even more so now after all the exercise in the fresh air.

Yesterday we attended a lecture given by our Medical Officer Lieut. Wakefield who explained the use of the gas helmet. Doctor Wakefield in his usual interesting manner gave us many good hints in reference to the German gasses and how to avoid them.

Mr. Kieley of the "Nickel" has a man here with a moving picture machine, he is taking views of the Newfoundland Regiment, on the march, bayonet exercise, skirmishing, etc., so you people will all have an opportunity of seeing us as we are. I hope they got a view of Lord Kitchener reviewing us, as it is worth having — wise man, Mr. Kieley. Captain Carty had his Company, A. Company, taken separately yesterday evening, perhaps B. Company may also have a separate picture. Capt. Carty never loses an opportunity to do the boys a good turn, for he takes great interest in all under him. Long may he be with us!

Bruce Reid is promoted Corporal. This is a very popular promotion, for he is a splendid fellow — a thorough gentleman — and everybody expresses the hope that he will have a commission very soon, for amongst all the commissions given it is peculiar that Bruce was not one of those promoted. When we think of all the Reids have done for the Regiment and for Newfoundland, it is only proper that a son of theirs should hold the highest position possible in "Ours."

Kind regards to all friends; tell them that we hope to do our best when get in the firing line.

THIRTEENTH LETTER

Aldershot,

August 17, 1915.

UST A LINE OR TWO on the eve of our departure for the Dardanelles. The King is coming today to inspect us and wish us God-speed, and we leave tomorrow for Southampton to embark. Today we have all been fitted out with new uniforms, as those we have been using are too warm for out there. We now have been given very thin cotton stuff, khaki colour, and khaki helmets. I can tell you we look some stylish in that rig. No doubt you will be seeing views of us. The helmets are far ahead of the caps we've been wearing, "perfect dreams," (ahem!) I expect all the ladies in Newfoundland will be having their hats "Helmet shape" next season in honour of the Newfoundland battalion. When you are reading this we shall be far enough away, perhaps have landed at the Dardanelles, and may we all do our bit and bring further honour to Newfoundland. It will no doubt be some time before letters will be received from any of the Contingent, for it will probably take us two weeks to get to our destination, then the hurry and rush of landing, etc., etc., and a letter from the Dardanelles to

Newfoundland would take about three weeks, so nobody at home need worry if there are no letters from us until say five weeks' time.

All our transport men are busy now getting things under way. We have a lot of mules in addition to the horses, and of course some of those mules are as "stubborn as a *mule.*"

Capt. O'Brien arrived from Stob's this a.m., and is going to the front with us. He intended remaining with E. and F. Companies, but later arrangements transferred him back to us again, and never was any officer more popular with men than Capt. O'Brien. All the men in sight as he passed into barracks gave him three cheers, for he is so well liked by everybody — an efficient officer as well as a thorough gentleman.

All the boys are well and delighted at prospects of seeing the front and doing something. I shall hope to be able to send you an item or two as soon as we get settled, and, you bet, I shall be able to say that our Contingent are "right there with the goods." We are all determined to do our part, knowing that all you people at home are patiently waiting and watching for good news from us. Let me tell you that this regiment will do good work for they are thoroughly fit — every man.

Now we have to say good-bye to Aldershot and after a brief stay, good-bye to England; we hope to meet some of the kind friends again we have met in Scotland and England.

I will write as soon as possible after we land in Egypt.

FOURTEENTH LETTER.

On board R.M.S. *Megantic*,
Lemnois, Dardanelles, Aug. 25th.

OU WILL BE GLAD TO KNOW that "Ours" has arrived safely at the base, and perhaps readers of the *News* would like to hear about our trip, therefore I will give a few notes extracted from my diary, but before I begin let me say this letter will probably have to pass through the censor's hands before being forwarded, and I am not yet sure as to what we can mention and what we have to leave out, therefore you will understand if the words are erased in some places. I hope the Censor will be a little easy and let as much go as possible, as all the folk at home, I have no doubt, would like a little account of our very interesting trip. Well, here goes. Now, where's that diary?

Aug. 19th — Left Aldershot at 8 p.m., all excepting balance of E. Company, (not transferred), and all of F. Company — they go back to the depot — Ayr. The people turned out in good style and gave us a great 'send off,' and a couple of bands from some of the English regiments played us to the station, and so away we went in full marching order, with kit and blanket, amid the cheers and good wishes of the people of Aldershot.

Aug. 21st — About 4 p.m. the train stopped at Exeter and some waiters come forward to the doors of each carriage and handed every man a package containing a sandwich, a piece of cake, two apples and a package of cigarettes with a card, saying: "With the compliments of the Mayoress of Exeter" and in addition to this they gave each man a cup of coffee, "hot, strong and sweet." How good of them! Then the doors were shut and on we went and arrived at Devonport 8:30 a.m. The train brought us right to the pier, and there lay the magnificent steamer *Megantic* awaiting us. What a splendid system they have for embarking troops, not the least disorder. We went on board in single file, and as each man stepped over the gangway he was given a ticket with number of room, also number of berth, so there was no trouble for him to know where he had to go. Then we had breakfast and for our meals we were each given a ticket, 'first', 'second' or 'third' sitting, as the case may be, as all cannot sit down at once — then, in addition to our regiment, about a thousand 'Royal Warwickshires' embarked also, going out the same as ourselves. We lay at the pier all day. At 6:30 p.m. tugs came along and we moved out, and as we moved and began to get under way, the tugs left us, and at the same time two great torpedo destroyers fell in with us, one on our starboard and the other on our port bow, as much as to say "Don't worry, we are going to see you safely out of the danger zone," and can't those destroyers go? Well "some!" for our ship is fast (can do twenty-four knots when required), but these

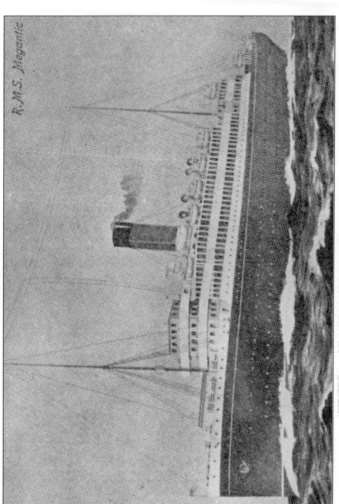

R.M.S. Megantic

HM. TRANSPORT SHIP *MEGANTIC*

guardians of ours simply held on to us until we were away off the coast into the open sea, then they left, and we understand other escorts will meet us at the entrance to the Straits of Gibraltar.

At 11 a.m. we had to fall in with life belts on, for boat drill. There is a life belt for every man kept in his berth, and the boats are all swung out with oars, etc. ready for lowering at an instant's notice. Every man is allotted to some boat, and it is his duty to fall in on the deck nearest his boat, and lose to time about it, consequently, should anything happen, we are all ready to make the jump. I hope we will not need to take to the boats, but we are prepared in case some of the German pirates do get a chance at us. At night everything is quiet, no lights are allowed and the greatest precautions are necessary; it is watch, watch all the time. Besides our machine guns the ship is fitted with a 'four point seven' on her quarter, and the Germans will get a warm time, and it is so warm. I don't think I ever say anything about all of us being fully armed, ready for the first call, because the Censor might cross it out, and I don't want these notes too much like 'dots and dashes.'

Aug. 22nd — Another glorious day, not a cloud, the sea so calm, sun shining bright; indeed it makes a fellow feel it is good to be alive. I went on deck at 5:30 a.m. We have to wear canvas shoes or bare feet all the time, and it is so warm. I don't think I ever saw anything finer than these two days.

After breakfast another boat drill, the alarm is given, unexpectedly of course, and away we dash. You may just bet your life we get there too in double quick time. And after that as there is not any more parade before dinner the men scatter about the decks playing games of one kind and another, the Newfoundlanders and Warwicks mixing together. We are great chums already, and I hear the familiar "Top o' the 'ouse.' Number 87,' 'Kelly's eye'," and so on. Then the games continue, with everybody happy, Germans or Turks don't worry this bunch — "not much."

Retired at 9 p.m., a glorious night but very warm, and they tell us it will be warmer still as we go along, and at our destination it is as hot as — Phew! let's think of something else.

Aug. 23rd — Up at 5 a.m. Same beautiful weather and so calm. Well what a lovely trip we are having. My arm is a little sore to-day from inoculation yesterday. I forgot to say we were all inoculated yesterday against cholera. I expect we are fairly well fortified now against any disease that may come along, for since joining the regiment all have been inoculated against typhoid, then vaccinated against smallpox, and now this for cholera. Wish someone would invent some kind of inoculation against German submarines, but that may come later. We are still keeping up our eighteen knots. This ship does plough through the water and the German pirates will have to go some to catch us. We passed several steamers and we have come so far and no sign of anything in the shape of any enemy. Oh, yes, 'Britannia does rule the waves.' No sign of land yet although we expected to be at Gibraltar by this. Somebody said that owing to warning about enemy submarines in the vicinity our ship has "hove off" about 150 miles. At about 8:30 p.m. lights from lighthouses are seen on our starboard and port, this no doubt is the Spanish coast on our left and Algiers on the right. Beautiful night indeed, as every night has been since we left, and I was sorry when 9 p.m. came and the usual order 'all troops to their quarters,' for I would like to stay on deck longer. However, away to the land of dreams now.

Aug. 24th — On deck at 5:30 a.m. and it is another glorious day. We passed Gibraltar last night. I thought we might have stopped there. Possibly we will stay a few hours at Malta. Passed several steamers today, this ship seems to pass everything, nothing so far has been able to keep up with us. Land on our starboard all day, (Africa-Morocco), it is good to see land or ships, now and again; makes it more interesting. Stayed on deck until the last minute this evening, saw several lights from the lighthouses on the coast.

Aug. 25th — Just before noon passed large steamer, going in our direction escorted by two destroyers, one ahead and one astern. Our ship hoisted the ensign. Just heard that the steamer we saw is an Austrian with six thousand tons ammunition for the Turks, and was captured by the French. The destroyers both display the French flag. Well done France. After tea went on deck again for another smoke of "Mayo's" and see the sights. Found it very warm in stateroom last night; have decided to sleep in smoking room tonight, and at 9 p.m. I proceed to do so.

Aug. 26th — Nothing unusual yesterday. Another fine day; arrived at Malta 11:30 a.m. Pilot boat came out to us. Malta is a beautiful place, sorry we could not get on shore. Lots of Maltese bum boats came out to us and pestered us to death to buy their wares, chocolates, cigars, etc. but the police boat from the city cleared them away. They are not allowed to sell to troops for various reasons. Little Maltese boys came alongside, and for a coin they would dive and bring it up in their teeth, it is great fun to watch them.

Aug. 27th — Left Malta at 9 a.m. and had a great run, but we are now in the most dangerous part of our voyage. A destroyer escorted us out and away we went. During the day we passed several islands, and many ships, French and British.

Aug. 28th — At 8 a.m. arrived at our present destination. This is the base, and a torpedo destroyer came out and escorted us to our anchorage. I wish I could tell you the sight before my eyes at the present moment, as I sit on deck, this beautiful harbour, and so much of interest here, but I know the Censor would erase it, so it will have to wait until we return. This must end this part of our travels. You know where we are now and what it means. We are all well and everybody happy. Just think of Our regiment doing their bit; and doing it successfully and well from now on, for the real thing lies before us. May we do our duty nobly and well, and bring honour to 'Ours' and to Newfoundland.

P.S. — Since writing the above the ship has been ordered to Alexandria, and we are to go also, presumably to be brigaded. Will write when we get settled.

FIFTEENTH LETTER.

———

Cairo, Egypt,

Sept. 7th, 1915.

HEN I WROTE LAST we were at Lemnois, Dardanelles, but ordered to Alexandria and from thence to Cairo arriving here Sept. 2nd at 5 a.m. So you see we have been moving a bit since leaving Aldershot. Lemnois is interesting, it is a base of operations in the Dardanelles. We anchored close by the shore, where so many troops were put out of business when landing at the first of the war with the Turks. No doubt you remember about that. When the soldiers were being rowed ashore the Turks were concealed and opened fire on the boats, and many a poor fellow died without even touching the land.

Well we have been, we may say, to the scene of many a fight during the first of the war. Now the Allies have forced their way along and Lemnois is now used as a base, filled with warships, British, French and Russians, and several hospital ships and many 'prizes.' We were fully prepared to land, each man fully armed and pouches filled with ammunition, and even water bottles filled when orders came for us to go to Alexandria, and now here. We are camped "next door" to some

Australians, and when they heard we were 'Colonials' you just bet they couldn't do enough for us. Go where you like in Cairo now, and the usual sight is several Newfoundlanders and several Australians together. Never two lots of individuals were more friendly. They are simply crazy about the Newfoundlanders, and our crowd are the same over them. No doubt about it those chaps from the biggest island in the world have the best hearts in the world, the jolliest lot we've struck yet, and you don't need me to tell you about the part the Australians played in the Dardanelles, for all the world knows what they've done; the Turks call them "the white Ghurkas," and are just scared to death over them.

I think I said just now 'we are in Cairo.' Well I guess so, and we are not likely to forget this trip. We've seen sights going through Scotland and England and will never forget the wonderful things seen there, but this place simply beats all. At first we were amused, then we got serious, and now — well now we are at a standstill — aghast — don't know what to think of it. You've only to look through an illustrated Bible and see the sights we see every day here, the man astride his camel going over the sands, and the streams of people on asses, people about in the streets, some lying and some kneeling, sometimes asleep, other times eating queer looking food with unpronounceable names. Bootblacks are as thick as flies, and that is saying a lot, and they will insist on cleaning a fellows boots, no use to say 'No.' The people seem to be all over the place, in the shady spots from the sun. Talking about the sun, oh! dear me! we do get the full benefit of it here, the heat is fierce, too hot for parades in the middle of the day, so we have them always before sunrise and after sunset, and during the day we have all we can do to fan the flies off us. We parade at 5 a.m. until 9, and from 4 p.m. until 6, or perhaps later, according to the distance we go. The tents are different from any we used in the Old Country. These are made expressly for hot countries, they have double roofs.

Cairo is of about four hundred thousand population, and as you know, one of the most interesting cities in the world, and during the "season" in Cairo (from November until May), visitors from all parts of the world are to be seen mixed with picturesque natives. The money here is funny to us but we are getting used to it now. They have "piasters." One piaster is worth two-pence half-penny or five cents. They have up-to-date street cars, and the fare is a quarter of a piaster, and go as far as you like, quite cheap isn't it? But wages are very cheap, so that accounts for prices, for instance, the average wage for labourers here is one piaster per day, that is five cents per day, and nobody on strike.

The distance from Alexandria to Cairo is 133 miles and it is a pity our train travelled by night for we lost the beauty of the trip, for on both sides of the cars on the way grow palms, dates, bananas, Indian corn, sugar cane, etc. The natives of Cairo are rather scared of the white soldier, even to the native policeman, who touches his hat to us. I tell you I felt quite elated the first day I walked through the city, when at every corner the policeman saluted me. The natives will bother white people quite a lot if you give them any scope, then if you roar "Rooh fi dalua," just watch them scatter.

There are some wonderful old buildings here. One University, the "Mosque El Ayar" was built 988 A.D., and has about 15,000 students from all the Mohammedan centres. Then the wonderful old mosques and burial places, hospitals, etc. One mosque was built 680 A.D. The Coptic Church (old Cairo), is on the spot where the Virgin Mary hid with her son from Herod, this is certainly worth seeing, and at Materiyeh, a village close by, is the sycamore tree under which, legend says, the Virgin rested with the infant Jesus on her flight from Herod. I visited the Pyramids yesterday, and that is something to remember in the days to come. Natives took us there, we went on camels' backs. Just imagine us going along on those queer looking animals, they charged five piasters (twenty-five cents) for the trip, which is cheap, for the unique ride on a camel is alone worth twenty-five cents, (but give me a horse after this please). One Pyramid, "The Great Pyramid" was built 3733 B.C. The contents of stone to make this are calculated to be no less than ninety million cubic feet; the top is about thirty-five feet square and it is 465 feet high; it took twelve years to construct a road, and no less than a hundred thousand men toiled for about twenty-two years in erecting this Pyramid, and let me say in passing, I am surprised they built it so quickly, for I've seen the natives about here working and goodness me they "go some," case of "come day, go day, God send Sunday." The other Pyramids were built about the same time.

Heliopolis, close by, is the residence of the Khedive. "Heliopolis" is built on the site of ancient Heliopolis," or "City of the Sun," in whose temples thousands of priests officiated. There used to be a large community of Jews here, and from them Joseph chose his wife who was the daughter of the priest Potipherah. Reminds one of Sunday School days. There is also an obelisk, sixty-six ft. high, erected 2433 B.C., and solemn thoughts came into our minds as we stood at the foot of this Obelisk erected so long ago.

The museum here is worth seeing. I am going there tomorrow, as when a fellow gets an opportunity to visit a country like this it is worth while taking it all in, or all that we possibly can.

Don't know how long we shall be here, perhaps only a few days more, as we are only here to get a little bit climatized, then Turks look out.

Do you remember me mentioning a young man named Gilbert in our Regiment, in the same tent as we were at Stob's? He received a commission and got transferred to a Welsh regiment. We got word a few days ago that he had been killed in the Dardanelles. Poor fellow, it is very sad, and he was such a splendid chap.

Wish I had time to tell you more about Cairo and surroundings, the wonderful desert, the petrified forest and Moses's well, the great tombs, churches, statues, museums, etc., but it will have to wait for another date. With kindest regards to all friends. Tell everybody we are all well.

SIXTEENTH LETTER.

Somewhere in the Dardanelles,
September 27th, 1915.

I AM WRITING THIS IN MY "DUG-OUT," perhaps you know what that is, and possibly some of your reader's don't. A "dug-out" is a place dug in the ground large enough for a man to lie down, and sometimes after going down three or four feet or more we dig in, and make a cave, and there we may lie back comfortably and fill our pipe with 'Mayo,' if we have any, and smile at the shells bursting on the roof overhead.

At present the shells are coming fast and thick, some whistling by, others bursting somewhere where we might be but for this very convenient "dug-out." If it were not for the dug-outs we would have to stay in the open ground exposed until a shell dropped near us, and then we would likely go somewhere else — in sections — which would be rather unpleasant.

We have had quite a lively time since landing Monday morning amidst a storm of shot and shell. After reaching the shore we made a rush and getting out our trenching tools began to dig ourselves in. The shells were falling thick about us. Lieut.

Nunns was orderly officer that day, and a trying time he had of it rushing here and there. He must certainly bear a charmed life, for he did not stop, but went about from one man to another, seeing to everybody, and the wounded falling sometimes quite near.

About twenty-five of our fellows were hit, including the Adjutant, Capt. Rendell, but only one was killed, young McWhorter of Bay of Islands. It is greatly to the credit of Newfoundland the way our boys behaved under fire. One would think they were old soldiers, and it is wonderful that more were not injured, as there were some narrow escapes. One shell burst about five feet from our dug-out; we only just "ducked" in time. Another knocked Sergt. Green's helmet off, and it went about twenty feet away. He has never seen it since. Lieutenant Nunns nearly got knocked out several times, but he held on until at last we had to move to another spot "somewhere" more safe. We went into the trenches next day and came out last night and go back again this p.m. or tomorrow.

Our chaps acted splendidly in the trenches during the seventy-two hours spent there. "Some" trench I can tell you. I wish I could tell you all about it, but there, I cannot now. Poor Frank Hardy of A Company was shot in the head by a bullet, and yesterday Jack Blyde received a shot in the head. Poor fellow he only lived a few hours. This is the third death in action. Jack Blyde belongs to B Company, and I was not far from him when he fell. One of the men of the Hants, (English regiment) was shot at the same time. He was next to me at the time he received the bullet. Lieut. Nunns again distinguished himself, but narrowly escaped death several times. Once the periscope was knocked out of his hand by a bullet, another bullet struck the plate containing the lookout through which he was peeping at the time, but, nothing daunted, he got a rifle and I think he accounted for a good many Turks.

Brother Stenlake also played his part well one night out sniping Turks, and I guess he bagged a few. I was sent out to the advance trench one evening with two other fellows, and three from a Dublin regiment in charge of a Dublin Sergeant. I tell you it is good to hear a bit of real Irish after all the English and Scotch, and these chaps are fine fellows; they fear nor care for anything. Once, when looking through the periscope, a bullet crashed through the top of it and knocked it out of my hand, but these little things will happen, for they say that during the South African war it took about three ton of ammunition for every man killed, so I ought to have something over two tons to pass yet.

A shell has just burst about three feet above our dug-outs, nobody hurt, and Sergt. McLeod, who has his dug-out a couple of "doors" away, doesn't look as if he worried, as he now sits eating his lunch with a smile on his face, shells or no shells. Sergt. James is near him shaving; another cool hand. Shells don't worry Jimmy or Mac.

Stenlake just strolled over to my dug-out. I said, "Why aren't you under cover old man, you will be hit if you're not careful?" "Oh," he said, "I was just trying to see if I could not arrange a short service this afternoon as it is Sunday." Just imagine — but that is Stenlake all over. His idea, I think, if he were to express himself, is "shells and bullets of course are rather awkward to have dropping about you, but having a word of prayer, even in the jaws of death, is more important."

Just a few feet from the dugout is a grave with a rough wooden cross, and on it "Lieut. W.E. Norris, 25 August, 1915." Another near it says, "In memory of an unknown comrade." Young McWhorter and the other two of our boys were laid away to rest amongst many noble men who have within a short space of time given their lives for King and Country.

I wish I could tell you more about this spot, but I cannot. If I could tell it, I am sure it would make many a young man feel ashamed to be loafing around at football matches, when he should be in the trenches. I must close now, as this is not very convenient for writing letters, but will drop a few lines again when I get an opportunity.

Tell all at home that we are doing our best to bring honour to Newfoundland and they need not be a bit ashamed of the first Newfoundland Regiment.

SEVENTEENTH LETTER.

———

In the trenches,
"Somewhere in the Dardanelles,"
October 13th, 1915

HIS IS OUR NINTH DAY IN THE TRENCHES and our third "go" at the wily Turk. It is said that we move out to our dug-outs tomorrow for another rest — "a Newfoundland spell," viz: we rest by day and go digging at night, and then back again to our 'little grey home in the trench.'

Last time we were relieved by our old friends, the Munsters. We have made many friends amongst these Irishmen, and they are certainly 'the boys.' You ought to see them in action. We have met many soldiers from different parts of the Empire, but those Irishmen simply are the limit, very alert, full of go, with nerves that beat all. They are up to every trick of the Turks, and the Turk is tricky. It is a pleasure, if I may so express myself, to be holding a trench with those chaps, they inspire confidence in everybody — excepting the enemy.

Let me give you one little instance — one of the many — that shows that the Irishmen are "right there with the goods." The other day six of us, three Newfoundlanders and three Munsters in charge of a Munster Sergeant, were sent out in front of our trench, a very dangerous position, to guard a new sap and, whilst there, one of our chaps espied a Turk through the periscope quite plainly. The Turk was standing in a hole with about half of his body visible. We got our rifles ready to fire, when the Irish Sergeant said, "Don't shoot boys, that's just a trick of Johnny Turk. You don't know them as well as I do, for," he said, "they only want to draw our fire. They have an idea somebody is here, and doubtless a couple of their sharp-shooters — 'snipers' — are hidden close by with their rifles trained on this parapet waiting for us to poke our heads up to shoot, and before we would have time to press the trigger they would have us." So we let Mr. 'decoy' Turk severely alone that time. This is only one instance to show that the Turks have got to "go some" to get over our friends from the Emerald Isle, for inexperienced soldiers at that time would have "blazed" away or attempted to, with a disastrous result to our side. Oh, we cannot but admire those Irish soldiers.

Now I must tell you about the Irish priest. In an advance here a little while ago, this priest, a young man, was in the very front of the battle, attending to the wounded, not caring a bit about himself, and when wounded twice, he was begged by the other officers to go to the rear. He replied, "No, my men need me and here I stay." He was wounded again and again, yet refused to go to the rear, and at last he fell dead. They found nine wounds in his body. There was a hero! We often read about such heroism, but all the heroes are not in story books, or newspapers either, and if anybody doubts me let them come to the Dardanelles for a few weeks. Lots and lots of stories such as this never are published, but when this war is over and all are settled down calmly, men who have participated will tell of very many deeds of valour. Things are going on here, and in Flanders too, that people never dream of at home. You may quite believe it that all the brave men did not live in olden times.

Since last writing we have had a few more casualties. Sam Lodge was killed, shot through the side. He only lived a few minutes. He was an excellent fellow, and we all miss him. Dave Carew, another, was shot through the head. Hardy (in D Co.) was shot through the head but is still living. Lieut. Gerald Harvey was shot in the chest, and is in the Hospital. He will be O.K. after a couple of months, also Lieut. Carter, who got it in the knee, and will be disabled for some time, but no doubt you have the official list before this.

Up to the present as near as I can judge, we have, besides sick, about sixty wounded and eight dead. Two of our fellows died of dysentery, — Lance-Corporal Watts of A Co., and Pte. Walter Murphy of No. 8 Platoon, B Company. Walter was in our platoon and we all miss him so much, such a quiet unassuming fellow, he was liked by everybody. His brother, Mike, is in C Company.

We won't be sorry to get to the dug-outs tomorrow for a brief rest. We look forward with pleasure to the fact that tomorrow night we may take off our boots when retiring. Oh, delicious thought, it makes us happy all over, and if any of your readers want to get a small idea of what a comfort it is, just let him sleep in his clothes, in his comfortable bed, not in a trench, for say two days, not two or three weeks, and ask him how it feels, — yes, even to remove his boots only. Some day no doubt we will be able to remove our tunic and pants, and yes, perhaps, our shirt, and even have a wash. When that time comes I shall certainly have to ask somebody to pinch me to make sure that I am not dreaming.

We read with pleasure about the thousands of socks, mufflers, and shirts the good people at home are sending. God bless them. We wish somebody would invent vermin-proof shirts, for the Turks are not the only vermin we have to do battle with out here.

I suppose you are having cold weather at home now. We have it very warm by day and very cold at night. Summer weather all day and winter at night. One consolation is that at night the flies leave us, for they are numerous during the heat of the day, and when eating our meals, if we open a tin of jam we have to eat it quickly, or the flies will do so for us. Soon the rainy season sets in, and the "cheerful" old veterans tell us it means weeks and weeks of rain. No doubt they will provide us with rain-proof coats, and long boots long before that. Last night we had a shower, quite heavy for about half an hour. We put our rubber sheets over us, and it wasn't so bad.

"Somewhere" in Gallipoli,
October 14th.

ACK TO OUR DUG-OUTS. Came down last evening after all, and we had a decent sleep last night "with our boots off." Jack Brett and I occupy the one dug-out, and about 2 a.m. it rained to beat the band. Fortunately we had "rigged" up our rubber sheets over head, which kept it off a bit. In the dark I got up and hung up a pair of boots over my feet to keep the rain off. In the morning on investigation, I found the boots filled with water, and to make matters worse (for Jack), we discovered it was his boots, not mine, that I had hung up in the darkness. However the sun soon dried them. Jack is one of the best shots in our Company, and this reminds me. Sunday in the trench we saw a Turk and his dog, (they use dogs to carry food and ammunition to their snipers), and Jack got ready to fire just as the Turk went into his dug-out. He got the dog full in the shoulder, and doggie was "strafed," and that Turk's food supplies cut for one twenty-four hours at least.

They say Bulgaria has joined Turkey, but it is not of any avail, for the destination of the British is Constantinople, and it is only a matter of time. I wish I could tell you more but the censor has to read this. You often hear people say, "What about the Navy? What are they doing?" Well, I wish those critics could come out here for a few days. They would not ask any more. Oh, I could tell you so much. Why only yesterday — Oh excuse me Mr. Censor, I nearly gave the show away.

Now lots at home are wondering about our boys, how each one is getting on. I wish I knew all individually, and had time and opportunity to write about them, but all are doing their part well, no shirkers, and Capt. Carty is certainly an inspiration to every man. He knows everybody and is continually going up and down the trenches with a word of cheer and encouragement for each one. It is "Hello Jack or Tom, how are you?" etc. God bless Capt. Carty. Everybody has something good to say about him.

Our feeding is good in the trenches, far better than one would look for in the firing line, but B Company., at any rate, is certainly fortunate in having Heber Wheeler in charge of the cooks. Nothing daunts him. His idea is to get good hot tea for the men, and other things nice. Nobody but Hebe himself knows the trials and troubles to get this done under the conditions, but we never miss a meal, although time after time they have been "shelled" out of the cooking place. Hebe yesterday held on until the last minute when a shell landed in the fire and sent dixies and fire all over the place. Then he ran, but do you think we did not have our tea as usual? Not at all, for with wonderful patience — and not a bit of fear — he began all over again, and nobody went without the usual meal.

Then we have Tom Humphries, Mess Orderly in Chief

for B. Company. He ought to be appointed M.O.E., (Mess Orderly Extraordinary) for the Regiment. Here's a true story about Tom, I saw it happen myself. Tom saw some watermelons between our trenches and the Turkish trenches, and concluded they would be a nice addition to the breakfast (lots of fruit about here), and without a word he climbed over the parapet and walked out right towards to enemy, picked several watermelons, and came back safely with bullets flying all about. When he went we begged him not to, but he did not flinch a bit. Why only a few days ago one of the K.O.S.B.'s got recommended for the D.C.M. for going out between the trenches and burning some dead Turks that there was not time to bury. We have had some narrow escapes amongst our fellows. Private Hodinott, when picking up a wounded man, felt a sting in the crown of his head, and discovered that a bullet had gone through his helmet and just grazed his skull. Will Taylor had a bullet rip through the collar of his tunic and not do him a bit of harm. Half an inch the other way, or less, would have done for each of them. R.C. Grieve had a bullet in his cheek, a nasty wound, but he will be O.K. in a few days

We are supplied with tobacco and cigarettes once a week, sent by good people in England, as, of course, it is impossible to buy anything here. If a fellow had a hundred pounds in his pocket it is useless to him, for there is nowhere to buy. If we have a pencil, a comb, or anything whatever we must take every care not to lose it, as there is no way to obtain more. I was fortunate enough to preserve a few sheets of paper and a bottle of ink, but that is almost finished. When we are all out I

MRS. ELIZABETH LIND, OF LITTLE BAY,
AND THE LATE HENRY LIND
Parents of Frank T. Lind

suppose they will supply some more, if not then we shall only have to rely on those heartless "deaf and dumb" postcards which tell no news, — just "I am well," or "I am wounded," as the case may be. Whilst I am writing the 'Turkish Delights' — as we call their shells — are bursting all over the place, but we are quite secure in our dug-outs, but, you bet, the Turks are not having it all to themselves. They are getting better than they sent every time. Oh, just wait until Christmas — for we will be eating our Christmas dinner in Constantinople.

Q.M. Sergt.-Major Hector McNeil is stationed in his dug-out down by the ———— oh! pardon again, Mr. Censor, I nearly said it. I was down before last trip to the trenches to get something out of my kit bag, and there we saw him assisted by Corporal Charlie Edgar and his staff, digging himself in, and at the same time dodging Turkish shells. One shell had just landed and torn away the work of three days, beside breaking two jars of lime juice and striking a suit of uniform belonging to Geo. Heath, and tearing it to pieces. George had just taken off the suit to have it repaired, but it is only fit for mat rags now. The piece of shrapnel simply dissected it. He is keeping the suit to bring back as a souvenir. I am sure none of us envy Q.M. Sergt. McNeil and his staff there, but they all seem quite happy, and when we left to go back to our dug-outs they had just begun to repair damages.

Lieut. Nunns had another narrow escape, a bullet grazed his eye making a scar. Had it been a quarter of an inch further to the left No. 8 platoon would have been minus their commander, but Mr. Nunns did not give up. He simply had his eye bandaged, and went about his duty as usual. I expect more than one Turk paid the penalty of that scar with his life, when Mr. Nunns got his sniping rifle going a few minutes after.

Lady Hamilton, wife of Sir Ian, is making us all a present of chocolate this week. Chocolates and cakes are very much appreciated by men in the trenches. Sweetmeats taste so much better under the conditions than they would at home. Many parcels of cakes, sweets, cigarettes, etc., sent our fellows from friends at home and in Scotland have never been received. It is a shame. Somebody must be getting the benefit of them. One of our chaps had a letter from his mother in St. John's, Newfoundland, saying she was sending him 200 cigarettes and three pairs of socks. He received the wrapping of the package and note inside, "From mother to ———" but no sign of the cigarettes or socks. Somebody I suppose thought they had a better right to them. Some friends in Edinburgh wrote me — I received the letter on arrival here — saying, "We are sending a parcel containing some cigarettes, cakes, etc." Never a sign of the parcel yet. I know of dozens of chaps who have had parcels sent them which they never received. Surely there is something wrong somewhere and the people who would rob a man who is in the trenches offering his life for his country ought to be stood against a wall and have the Newfoundland Regiment fire at them at ten paces — but let me stop grumbling.

Another of our chaps just wounded, Lance-Corporal Tucker, son of Mr. Tucker, Horwood Lumber Company., but I am glad to say it is not serious. (Unhappily it proved fatal and young Tucker passed away twelve days later. -ED.)

We are all being issued with another blanket today. That is good, for it is very cold at night, and we shall need all the warm clothing we get from now on. All were under the impression that it was very warm in the Dardanelles, but not at all. Alexandria and Cairo are warm, but here it is cold enough at night, and will be even colder as the season advances.

Some of the letters received here from Newfoundland spoke of us being at Alexandria, and the people felt uneasy about us being "so near the firing line," but Alexandria is about 700 miles from the front. Why all the time in Scotland and England we were nearer the firing line than we were at Alexandria.

Lieutenant Summers, Quartermaster, is a very busy man. He hardly ceases night and day, and the result is the Regiment is always supplied with whatever is needed. Mr. Summers is certainly the right man in the right place.

I think I will "ring off" now, but will write again when I can. Kind regards to all friends. By the way it might be interesting to the young ladies at home who have sweethearts here in the Regiment to know that letters they send here are *not censored*, it is only the ones we send are *censored*, so it may relieve the minds of some of the dear girls to know they can put all the nice things they like on their letters, and rest assured that only THE man will read it. Now Terra Nova girls be happy and write all the nice things you wish and tell all the sweet dreams you have.

Before closing I would like to say that this war is likely to make a great change in the ways and customs of people in our own Island home, for the boys are so adept at entrenching and digging themselves in that, should two men, after we get back, have a quarrel on Water Street, no longer need they stand in the street and hammer each other, but away to Bowring's Cove and dig a trench and throw stones at one another; and again, the small boy's troubles in connection with seeing the football matches and other sports will be reduced to nothing. The burly policeman at the gate need no longer have any terror for him. All he will want is a periscope. He can then stand on the ground outside the fence of St. George's field and take in the whole show for nothing.

The boys wish to thank all kind friends who have sent them papers and magazines. I can tell you reading matter is very much appreciated here. It is so hard to get anything to read during any spare hours we have that all are glad when the Newfoundland mail comes in. Any old magazine, no matter what date, is grasped after and read and passed from one to another until it is worn out by usage.

Sorry to say so many of our chaps are ill in Hospital. Only about half the battalion is fit for duty, but we hope to see them about again soon.

NINETEENTH LETTER.

————

> "Somewhere" in the Dardanelles,
> October 30th, 1915.

 ES, WE ARE STILL "SOMEWHERE" IN THE DARDANELLES. I wish I could tell you exactly our position, in fact lots of things I would like to tell you, but alas I cannot. However, some day you will know all.

Poor Squibb lost his life last week in the trenches, shot through the head, but, no doubt, you have the official list, also of the others wounded, so there is no need for me dwelling on it.

We are back in the dug-outs again, new ones, after eight days in the trenches this last time, and we return again the day after tomorrow. The artillery from our batteries and the —— —— are continually sending shells screaming over our heads. Such a din — but we are quite used to it now. I wonder sometimes how those of us who go back to Newfoundland will be able to sleep comfortably without the continual boom ringing in our ears.

As usual when we are out for "rest" we have lots of fatigue work to do, digging, etc. One of the N.C.O.'s in our regiment had a dream the other night. He dreamt he was away back home, and the first thing he said was: "Father, you are number one, Mother number two, Uncle John three, and sister Mary four. Now mother and Mary must form fours. Father and Uncle John fall in with picks and shovels, and numbers two and four are on fatigue work in the cook-house, whilst I am going out in the back yard and get dug in." Then he awoke and found he was still 'somewhere in the Dardanelles.'

A Turkish prisoner just passed through our lines on way to a place where he will have little chance to do harm; he is in charge of two soldiers with fixed bayonets, and what a sorry sight the poor Turk looks, no boots, his clothes torn in many places, about the most "down-and-out" specimen we've seen yet. The only thing human we noticed about him was he had a cigarette in his lips, puffing away. Glad to say he didn't smile when passing us, for his face is so dirty it would be a horrible sight. The guards told us that when they caught him he was simply starving, and they suggested offering him some jam and bread, and opened a tin of jam. Well, one bun of bread and the contents of the tin disappeared in about five minutes, and likely the can itself would have gone if they hadn't taken it away. This is the state the poor Turk is driven to by those German officers. The Germans even chain the Turks on to the guns (artillery) so as they cannot retreat if they want to. It is awful. We all seemed to look down on the Turk, "the unspeakable Turk," but do you know they are far cleaner fighters than the Germans. They never use gas and in many instances they have attended to our wounded and given them cigarettes, and several times have been known to carry men of the British side back to the British lines after dressing their wounds. Just imagine the cultured (?) German doing this! And our Red Cross is always safe from their artillery. It is only the Germans that drive the Turks on. It is a case of go forward and be shot by our side, or retreat and be shot down by the German officers who dominate them. No wonder they appear quite happy when taken prisoner, knowing they will get enough to eat and be cared for.

We don't hear any war news worth while here, and have no idea of how things are going in Flanders or on the sea. Would you believe it, we get lots of news on our own home papers, although rather late, but news we cannot get here at all. So you can understand how much a home paper is looked for amongst us fellows.

It is a little warmer the past few days, but we dread the cold days and nights to come. Perhaps today it will change again, and then comes that rotten cold dampness for days and days. The people who fitted us out for a warm climate, when sending us here, had a poor idea of what it is like. I don't suppose there are ten men in the regiment who were lucky enough to have brought a pair of drawers with them. I hope you won't think I am complaining but I am sure I voice the sentiments of every man in the regiment when I tell you that we feel disgusted on looking through the St. John's, Newfoundland, papers and reading about so many thousand pairs of socks, thousands of underclothing, etc., being knitted by the good women at home for "our boys at the front." The question somebody asks every day is: "Where does it all go to?" for men in the Regiment are cold and wretched standing sentry at nights with perhaps one thin shirt under their tunic. I would shock you if I told the length of time most of the shirts have been on the men *since being washed.* Lots of them are wearing the same shirt put on either in Aldershot or en route. We have not received anything from the W.P.A. since the time we were at Fort George.

Now all along until we got to the front, none of the men bothered, as we were always in places where there were shops, and when a man wanted any clothing or anything he went and bought it, but here as I have already told you, we are isolated. Money is of no use, and if there were shops to buy things nobody would say a word. Are you aware that in the firing line in France the men spend, I understand, about forty-eight hours in the trenches and ninety-six hours out, but when out they have not dug-outs as we, but Y.M.C.A. canteens, stores, and houses to go to, and have a good feed, a bath, and all sorts of luxuries, and buy anything they need. Yet they seem to be getting the clothing that is so badly needed amongst our men. Don't think I exaggerate when I say "badly needed" for "the half is not told." I see things that would make your heart ache. Then of course, a soldier's life is rough, but why not make it as pleasant and comfortable as possible, — *and the winter is set in here.*

All the different Regiments here have their packages time after time sent from the country or city, as the case may be, which they represent; parcels of chocolates, cigarettes, and all sorts of things given by the people to their Regiment "at the front." For instance, the London Fusiliers have no end of stuff from London; the Royal Scots from Edinburgh, and so on.

The Royal Scots were near us last time we were out of the trenches, and when we met them they gave our fellows no end of cigarettes, candies, and in some cases pairs of gloves and mufflers, etc. They had more than they knew what to do with. Then the Australians, you ought to see the way they are looked after by their people. They need for nothing, and give piles of it away to whatever Regiments happen to be stationed near them from time to time, and those Australians are certainly 'gone' on the Newfoundlanders, ("Colonials, you know") they would do anything for our chaps. If we happen to meet up with any of them the word Newfoundlander bears a charm. It is, "Newfoundlanders ask what you will and you shall have it."

Sergt. Mansen is now senior N.C.O. of the No. 8 Platoon, Sergt. James being in hospital. Just now Lieut. Fox and Lieut. Shortall passed along on their way to ———— for a bath. You know them both, and they are excellent fellows. I'd like to know what A Company, or in fact any man in the Regiment wouldn't do for Jack Fox. He is certainly a very popular officer, always the same. He takes pleasure in doing anything for his men, and Lieut. Shortall seems to be following in the same footsteps, always a pleasant smile for everybody. And why wouldn't they be with such a good soul as dear old Captain Carty to guide them? Why most of the chaps look on Captain George Carty as a father, and he has proved a father to many a one in this battalion since leaving home. Lieut. Tait is back again, and we are all glad to see him. He is second in command in B Company; a splendid officer, and we trust he will remain with us, and that he will not feel any more a renewal of the sickness that gave him such bother. Sergt.-Major Paver is in hospital at Alexandria, and Sergt.-Major Sam Ebsary of A Company is now Battalion Sergt.-Major. Sergt. W. Clare is Company Sergt.-Major of A Company in his place. These two men fill the positions very well indeed, for both of them know their business from the word "go." But they are known in St. John's so well that any comment from me is unnecessary. Sam Ebsary, is well known in C.L.B. circles. Will Clare of the Cadets, familiarly known as "Bill," is one of the finest looking men in the Regiment, and as strong as an ox. I pity the Turk that falls into Will Clare's hands. It will certainly be "all day" with him.

Do you know Hubert Ebsary? He is the Corporal in charge of the Mess Orderlies of B Company, and the man who manipulates the jam and bacon in such a way that everybody has all that he requires. H. Wheeler, Arch Coombs, Jack Thompson, and Morris Carbery are the B Company cooks, and good ones at that. I told you about Hebe Wheeler last letter. Well, Arch Coombs has been in the Navy, and nearly all over the world, and even he admits that this is the "contrariest" and "cussedest" climate he ever struck. Then he is quite cheerful when a shell knocks all the dixies out of the fire. He gathers them up, and begins all over again. Abe Mullett had a narrow escape the other day. He was carrying a dixie of water to the cook house when a bullet plunked a hole through the dixie. All he said was "a miss is as good as a mile," and went off for a new dixie.

Our Colonel got wounded today, a bullet penetrating his

arm, which will put him out of business for some time. Lots of the places about here have been given names by different regiments, and in honour of the battalions fighting, such as Kangaroo Beach, named by the Australians; Anzac, Dublin's Valley, Borderer's Dump, and at the entrance to our dug-outs is a sign "Torbay" road; you can guess the origin of that, and the headquarters of the 88th Brigade to which the Newfoundland Battalion is attached, is called "Newfoundland Ravine." Quite an honour isn't it?

Tom Hammond of the Red Cross was mixing some drug in a bowl yesterday when a bullet went through the bowl without touching him; very near the mark. Another time, a few days ago in the trenches, a bullet went through Viscount's head — Viscount of D Company — and coming out struck Frank Somerton in the middle of his back penetrating his great coat, tunic and shirt, and making a scar in his flesh just enough to bring the blood. Of course the bullet was "spent" after striking the other man or Frank would have received a bad wound, perhaps lost his life. I could tell of scores of narrow escapes, yet in spite of it, everybody is as happy as can be. You cannot make the Newfoundlanders down-hearted — NO.

TWENTIETH LETTER.

———

Mudros,

Dec. 13, 1915.

 ORRY TO HAVE BEEN SO LONG without dropping you a line, but since last writing there has been "something doing" in more ways than one, and it seems tough after the splendid name "Ours" made for themselves in capturing "Caribou Hill", called after us, in which action Lieut. Donnelly won the Military Cross and Sergt. Green and Pte. Hynes got D.C.M.'s. I wish I had time to tell you all about it, and will do so as soon as I can, but, as I was saying, after that came, — shall I call it the "Deluge"? What a time we had. No doubt you've heard all official particulars but there is lots to tell yet; hundreds are in hospital with frost-bitten feet as a result of those awful nights and days, and many perished, though happily for Newfoundland, none of our Regiment. I am one of the number in hospital, but, thank God, the Turks had it worse than we, for whilst we beat around in ice water up to our waists, poor Mr. Turk had it up to his neck, and in many cases worse than that, for hundreds were drowned. Excuse short scribble, I am completely out of writing paper, but hope to get some here, as it is impossible to get anything at Gallipoli. Kind regards to all. I will write again soon. My feet are getting on well, but there are some bad cases. The doctors are very kind and do all they can for everybody.

Frank Lind in Hospital Uniform
Malta, March 3rd, 1916.

TWENTY-FIRST LETTER.

Floriana Hospital,
Malta,

Feb. 10, 1916.

OU SEE I AM "ON DECK" AGAIN after a long time. I wrote you a few lines from Mudros as I was about to go to England, but the ship only got as far as Malta, and was recalled to Salonika, so we were all put off here, and this is a fine place.

When last I wrote I was not feeling "in the pink." I can assure you, and have had rather a hard time since then; however I am now convalescent and hope shortly to be about again. I have no word of our regiment and do not know where they have moved to, and there seems to be no system about forwarding letters along. No doubt this is because the sick and wounded are scattered in the numerous hospitals here, also in Egypt and the Old Country.

No doubt you have heard all the news of our doings whilst in the firing line. I fear quite a lot of our fellows have been sent to hospital, sick and wounded, for the climate is certainly the "limit" and day after day would see many take the trek to the sea shore to embark for hospital. To give you an instance of the

numbers who had to be sent: — When we left Alexandria last
September for the Dardanelles the platoon which I belong to,
contained sixty-eight men, — good, solid men, in perfect
health — and when I left on the 10th of December for hospital
I left ONE MAN of that sixty-eight fit for duty. I was the
second last man knocked out; that is not counting the Mess
Orderlies and Cooks. George Butler was Mess Orderly that
time, and George is invincible, nothing seems to knock him
out; also Tom Mouland, another M.O., able to stand anything.

You have heard about the awful time we had in that storm.
I shall never forget the first night of it, when the rush of water
came through the trenches, carrying men, rifles and equipment,
provisions, etc., with it. Lance-Corporal John Luff proved a
hero during that trying time. Up to his waist in water he waded
about, and sometimes the water would be up to his neck and
over. At great risk to himself he plucked many fellows out of
danger as the ground was washed away with them, trenches
falling in everywhere. It was a rotten time, and we will never
forget Captain Alexander during that fearful storm. He and
John Luff seemed to be everywhere. Capt. Alexander worked
all of that night with the water almost up to his head, and
assisted by Corporal Luff used pick and shovel trying to
remove obstacles to allow the water to pass through. There was
nowhere to go; it was simply a case of "stick it" and let the rain
and snow soak through you. We stood it until about 4 a.m.
when Capt. Alexander again came towards us, I was going to
say floated towards us, for he was wading along with the water
up to his armpits. He had been fighting the waters all night, and

when he got near enough for us to hear his voice he said: "I am going to the cook house and have some hot tea made for you chaps." Not a thought about himself. He had been at it all night without a bite, and now at 4 a.m. he starts off to arrange a hot drink for his men. God only knows how he got to the cook house in that rain and darkness for he had to swim and crawl, but he got there and we reaped the benefit of his great goodness by having hot tea to cheer us up. Captain Alexander will never be forgotten by B Company for that action, as well as for many other times. He has shown that he thought of his men before thinking of himself. I almost forgot Sergt. Major Len. Stick; he worked like a Trojan during that storm, arranging for the men's comfort. Len is a good fellow, and never thinks anything too much trouble to do for the good of his men.

Now it is so long since I left the trenches that no doubt you have heard before this all about our experiences so it is no use for me to give it over again. Did you know that when I left the trenches our regiment had been *twenty-seven days* in the firing line — never to be forgotten days — twenty-seven days without taking off a stitch or having a wash. Oh, don't be scared, you "sit at home at ease nineteen to thirty-five-ers." We enjoyed it. Yes, really. You will think it incredible, but let the young fellows who think of enlisting believe me when I say that during those twenty-seven days we were as happy as anything. A fellow gets used to things, and conditions are not really as bad when a fellow says: "Well, I must make up my mind to put up with it." So you see, here I am, none the worse after all our hard time. Sure it is nothing after it is over. I had a Turkish shell that nearly removed my head one time, which I meant to bring with me, but in the rush I lost sight of it, for neither shells nor anything else bothered me when coming away. What a nice souvenir it would have made — a grand tobacco jar, for instance. Malta is a very interesting place — an island seventeen miles long and nine miles wide, inhabited away back in pre-historic times. The history tells us that the Phoenicians, probably from the neighbourhood of the Persian Gulf, came to Malta 1450 B.C. The island was then called "Malet" until about seven hundred years after the Greeks, who then occupied the island, called it "Melita," (meaning honey). Today, February 10th, is a general holiday in Malta — great doings in the way of processions, illuminations, etc., it being the anniversary of the shipwreck of St. Paul at Malta in 58 A.D., which led to the conversion of the Maltese to Christianity, and the Bay in which the prow of the vessel, the *Alexandrine*, struck is called St. Paul's Bay. There are some beautiful buildings in Malta. One, the Cathedral Church, is certainly worth seeing, built in 1700. All the altars and their frontages are made of marble, the high altar, that of the choir and those of the two side inner chapels being particularly remarkable for the rare marbles of which they are formed - Marble statues, beautiful paintings, etc., it is indeed worth a visit.

The Governor's residence is another magnificent building, built years and years ago, about 1572 A.D.

The Maltese are a somewhat different class of people from the Egyptians. They dress most respectably and are white. The women wear a black hood-like thing, mantilla, they call it, I think, over their heads. If they do not resemble the Egyptians in dress they certainly do in the *"What can I do for you?"* style. They out-do Egyptian and Turk in the money making, their chief motto in life seems to be "skin 'em" or "get money, honestly if you can, but get it." The most enterprising and unscrupulous financier will have to "go some" to out-do the Maltese in making money off others.

The population is about 220,000. The Governor is Field Marshal Lord Methuen, whose niece, daughter of Lord Pole-Carew, is one of the nurses here.

Before closing I must tell you about the milk "waggons" used in Malta. The milkman trots from door to door with probably ten or twenty goats following; the housewife passes out the jug for the milk, and the milkman simply milks the quantity required from one of the goats, and passes it back to the woman, who pays him. One thing she is sure of getting "fresh milk and no water in it." It is nothing strange to meet these milkmen going through the streets followed by their "staff" of goats.

TWENTY-SECOND LETTER.

———

Floriana Hospital,
Malta,

Feb. 28, 1916.

UST A FEW LINES to let you know I am getting along O.K. I am quite fed up with being in hospital, although we are treated so kindly. I hope they will soon consider me 'fit' enough to go back to the Regiment to be ready to do another 'bit.'

Captain Carty called to see me a few days ago. He was then making the rounds of Malta, looking up chaps belonging to the Regiment, for Capt. Carty takes great interest in the boys, and we are always glad to see him come around. Lieut. Sheppard also called a short time ago; he expected to be sent to Florence then. I understand that our Regiment is "Somewhere in Egypt." How hard it is to find out anything regarding where they are, yet no doubt you are getting word from them every mail in Newfoundland. I have not received a letter or paper since leaving the trenches. I suppose it is hard to trace a fellow when he is sent to hospital, there being so many hospitals.

We have quite a nice crowd in our ward, English, Irish, Scotch, Welshmen, Australians, New Zealanders, and, of course, last but not least (ahem!) yours truly, the only representative of the Ancient Colony in this hospital. Of course, there are quite a lot of our fellows distributed amongst the different hospitals in Malta, but I am the only one in Floriana. We have two Irishmen here, and one of them is certainly the born wit, the life of the place; his name is Loughnan of Dublin, who enlisted at the outbreak of the war; his business, (Commission Merchant) is carried on by his partner during his absence. I don't think we shall ever forget Mike Loughnan, for he knows everybody and everything, and can sing and dance and play the piano, act on the stage, in fact do anything at all. How I shall miss him; he ought to be in our Regiment, for he seems out of place here — "nuff sed."

When I spoke of the different characters we have here, I forgot to mention the Yorkshireman. Oh, dear me! "Thee baint gowin eet today, be thee?" which translated into English means: "Are you going out today?" One of them in the next bed to me is a very nice fellow ("he is, an' all") and we often have a chat, and actually I sometimes can make out what he says. Marvellous! And other times — oh, and other times, I just say "Yes" and "No," and laugh when he laughs; I understand then it is something amusing, but with all their funny way of speaking they are decent chaps. "They are, an' all."

I visited the Chapel of Bones last Wednesday. This is a very interesting place, but liable to give a fellow the creeps. The walls inside are composed of the bleached remains of those whose were interred in the burial ground attached to the hospital, years ago. There are arranged parts of the human body, many skulls, legs, arms. Such a sight! This peculiar piece of ghastly ingenuity was performed in 1852, by Rev. Sacco, the then Chaplain of the Hospital for Incurables. Well, I'd rather he have the job than I.

I went to see Tom Mouland of B Company, last week. He is in St. John's Hospital, with eleven shrapnel wounds. I could only see him then, but not speak, as he was very bad. I am going over again. Poor Tom, and I left him so well and strong, when leaving the Peninsula. I saw Joe Hurley also; he is at St. Patrick's Hospital, and is getting on all right. My old friend, Dan Des Roches, I just heard was at Cottoneria Hospital, with a bullet wound in the leg. I must try and see him today. A lot of our fellows are here somewhere. I must hunt them up.

TWENTY-THIRD LETTER.

Mustapha Camp,
Alexandria,

March 10, 1916.

LEFT MALTA SUDDENLY by the *Megantic* — our old friend — on March 4th. There are many of "Ours" here, about forty, waiting to be sent to join the regiment. The censorship is very strict just now, so that brevity is discretion.

TWENTY-FOURTH LETTER.

———

Mustapha Camp,
Alexandria,
March 16th, 1916.

 ERE WE ARE AGAIN. This is a Military Base Camp (it is military) for soldiers returned from hospitals where they are equipped, etc., ready for rejoining their regiment. I left Malta rather suddenly on the fourth of the month joining the *Megantic*, the same ship which brought us from England last August: ten of our chaps came by her, and on arriving here found about forty of our boys waiting to be sent to their units. When I left Floriana hospital they sent me to All Saints' Convalescent Camp, Malta, a lovely place by the sea shore, and in a direct line from our tent we could walk to the shore, (100 yards), and be in St. Paul's Bay, where St. Paul was wrecked — but we are not going to talk about St. Paul's wreckage now, we want to have a say about "Ours."

At All Saints' Convalescent Camp I found several of our fellows: Bob Sheppard, Corporal Pittman, J. Taylor and Mike Broderick, — more about Mike later. Well two days after I got to this Camp, they were making up a draft to send back to their units, and although I was supposed to stay there for a while and have a rest before being marked "fit," I managed to get put into the draft, as a fellow naturally wants to get back to his own, and away we went, about 200 from 'All Saints,' and various numbers from the different camps in Malta, making a total of 1800 for the troop ship, and when getting aboard we find it is our old friend the "*Megantic*," and meet many of the old hands, including the fellow who sold us ice water at a penny a glass last August.

I spoke of Mike Broderick just now, and although you have heard lots of the doings of "Ours" at the Peninsula there is much you have never heard — quite naturally — and when I met Broderick I thought of his little bit, done so quietly, for Mike never says a word himself. No doubt many of the people at home remember that Mike was one of the Quarter Masters on the S.S. *Newfoundland* two years ago during that terrible disaster, and although he was out in the storm all the time, where so many froze to death, Mike got off with only a frostburnt finger. So you can imagine that even that awful storm we had at the Peninsula had no terrors for Mike that first night, when the wind was blowing a hurricane, rain pouring in drops large as marbles, and the thunder and lightning making us think that the Last Day had come, and oh so dark! Well Broderick was at the Beach for rations and got caught in the storm on the way back; the transport carts sunk in the mud time and again, the mules did everything but turn themselves inside out, and it got so bad that the Indian drivers mutinied, and Mike had to force them at the point of his bayonet to "carry on." At last the drivers got away in the dark and "beat it" back, but our hero took the reins and drove the mules himself in the midst of that storm, hardly knowing which way to turn — but Mike has been in tough places before — and after beating about all night, he got to the trenches just before dawn. It is only an hour or so run in ordinary times. The result was the men of his unit had food for the next day of two. Had he gone back, what a state they'd have been in; this in only one of the many instances that Mike proved himself a man. I could tell you a score.

Another incident: Mike was sent down to Brigade Head-quarters to do some work for the General Staff, and proved a wonder by turning a cross-cut saw into a pit saw to saw timber, as they had no pit saw. The Colonel of the Brigade brought all his officers out to see the wonderful work done by this Newfoundlander, and Mike sawed under fire, men being killed all about him. Once, when Mike was on top at one end of the saw, the man under him was cut in two with a shell, and Broderick was looked on as a marvel by the others, when all he said was: "Put another man there in his place," and then went on sawing. Never came down! Well, to give you an idea that he bears a charmed life, he has three bullet wounds received during that time, and now is as well as ever. Simply "hard to kill," isn't he? The O.C. of the Brigade spoke well of Mike, and has even written him several times since he went to Malta. He looks on him as the wonder from Newfoundland, and he is a marvel, for he can turn his hand to anything; that is what surprises the English soldiers we meet, our fellows can do lots of things besides soldiering, and mind you we don't make bad soldiers either, eh, what? "Not 'arf!"

Sorry to hear Corporal Gallishaw is likely too ill to return to the Regiment, for he is such a splendid fellow; a real good sport. Just one instance about Gallishaw I will tell you, and then you'll want to pat him on the back the first time you see him. Always in good humour, I was near him when he got shot, and as he fell to the ground his first words were said with a grin: "That's a darn good shot whoever shot it." Such coolness, with the blood streaming out of him to joke like that. We did not know if we had better laugh or look serious, so we decided to laugh too, for that is the spirit Gallishaw seemed to put into everybody; his motto was: "Ah what odds, it might be worse." And then they brought the stretcher and away he went to the hospital ship, and the last I saw of him as the stretcher bearers turned the corner of the traverse good old "Gal." was puffing away at a cigarette, the same happy smile on his countenance. He is all grit from the word go, and I hope will come back to the Regiment again. Look at the way he stowed away on the ship to get to the front with the boys. You just bet we have some gritty chaps in our Regiment. I wish I had time to tell you all that I've seen and heard since leaving Aldershot; it would fill a book, for apart from the actions performed by the Regiment as a whole, the individual actions by different fellows, hundreds, are never known; some of them we hear part of, others are "born to blush unseen." What about the time big Mike Downey carried the wounded man out of the Turks' clutches back into the trenches? I wish you could have seen Capt.

Alexander, Len Stick and John Luff the first night of the flood, up to their waists in ice water wading about the trenches, and Captain Alexander ending it up by getting hot tea for the men that morning at 4 a.m. What a lovely — I mean lively — time we had, wet soaking through, blankets soaked as well and swept away. I remember after ninety-six hours in that trench, we got orders to walk "as you were," I mean "swim," back to the supports and try and dry our blankets, etc., and as we "floated" and plodded out through, every now and again some chap would get "stuck" and all had to turn and pull him out. I managed to hold on to my blankets until we got to the fifth traverse, when "I went to my chin," and still looking for bottom. Somebody gave me a hoist by the coat collar, but the blankets and ground sheet, "where, oh where are they now?" I held on to the rifle somehow or other, and my ammunition and equipment; of course, that was fastened to me, I couldn't get clear of it if I wanted to.

And now we are at Mustapha Camp with many other soldiers belonging to different units waiting to be sent to their regiments, and none of us will be sorry to leave Mustapha. This place, about three miles from Alexandria, is a beautiful spot; the sea shore is close by, and we bathe in the sea every day. Just the place to camp out; the tram cars run to town every few minutes. There is in fact, every convenience, a place where we ought to be perfectly happy, but for one thing. It is a place,

> Where every prospect pleases
> And only man is vile.

There are forty-five of our men here, all out of hospital during the last few weeks, and we wonder why we are kept here away from our Regiment. Following is a list of the victims "interned" at Mustapha:

Sergt. J. Robinson, Corporal F. O'Toole, Corporal W. Taylor, Lance-Corporal L. Bartlett, Lance-Corporal P. Daniels, Privates H. Andrews, J. Adams, M. Brien, S. Boone, J. Buckley, P. English, E. Gore, J. Hussey, H. Heath, T. Humphries, T. Janes, J. Kavanagh, F. Lind, J. Moore, W. Melee, A. Murray, C.P. Martin, J. McBay, D. McGory, R. Maddigan, J. Murphy, W. Power, C. Parsons, S. Penny, J. Pike, B. Ryan, W. Small, W. Snow, H. Seward, J. Squires, R.C. Sheppard, W. Taylor, W. Thompson, H. Thompkinson, A. Thompson, A. Webber, M. Walsh, E. Whitten, G. Warford, A. Young.

We all hope Lt. Col. Burton is back again with the Regiment, for he is so popular with the men and understands our fellows so well. Somebody said he was now at Cairo.

Sergt. John Robinson is senior of the Newfoundland Detail here and poor Jack, he would want fifteen heads on him to do all they want done. We hope and trust we will be moved to our Regiment soon.

Some of the boys were at Sidi Bishr a little while ago; that is a camp similar to this about five miles from here, and Sergt. Major Paver of our own Regiment being Senior Warrant Officer had charge, and it is good to hear the chaps tell about the way Mr. Paver looked after the Newfoundlanders. They were treated well because he appreciated what they had done.

I have received no letters since leaving the trenches, but I know there are some on the way for me, probably going to rounds of the numerous hospitals. The only things I received were eight packages of Christmas parcels which reached me the day before I left Malta, as they had gone to England twice, trying to find me out.

All the boys are going on O.K. and as happy as circumstances will permit. We are like chaps "interned" praying daily for release.

TWENTY-FIFTH LETTER.

A Mediterranean Port,

March 26, 1916.

 E HAVE ARRIVED HERE SAFELY FROM EGYPT going to join the Regiment "Somewhere in France." We have all the Mustapha crowd, and none are sorry to get out of that place. We arrived this a.m., on the S.S. *Lake Manitoba*. All well. The Germs. did not get an opportunity to practice their piracy on us. The Regiment has gone ahead of us.

TWENTY-SIXTH LETTER.

Somewhere in France,
April 21st, 1916.

MEANT TO HAVE WRITTEN YOU LONG AGO, but since coming here I have been laid up with influenza, in fact nearly everybody was affected, owing, no doubt, to the sudden change of climate, for there is such a difference between the air here and in Egypt. Before I begin, let me say that the censorship is very strict, all letters are read over and censored and anything not allowed is erased, so you will understand if every now and again you find a blank, but I shall try to steer clear of saying anything that will give the Censor trouble.

Well, we had a nice train run from Alexandria to Port Said; went on board ship on the eighteenth, found it was S.S. *Lake Manitoba*, a very slow boat, some difference to the *Megantic*. Owing to the presence of submarines outside we did not leave that day. The patrol boats and several cruisers spent the day and night, and all the next day (nineteenth) scouring the coast, then just at dark on nineteenth, feeling everything safe, we crept out, and on we went. We found out that the Regiment had

gone on a few days before. There were forty-five Newfoundlanders on board and lots of troops belonging to different
units, just out of hospital. No smoking was allowed on board
after dark. We had a gun on our quarter and found that the two
gunners in charge of it were Newfoundland N.R. men, as it is
always men from the Navy who are put in charge of guns on
troopships. Had we been chased by a submarine our only hope
was to blow her out of the water, as our speed would not allow
us to run away. The second day out they had target practice by
throwing empty boxes overboard, and when a long distance
astern firing at them. One of the gunners, Frye, hit the box both
times. He is an excellent shot. A strange thing occurred when
the first shot was fired without warning to anybody on board,
and the report of a canon aboard a troopship, when every
minute you expect a torpedo, is going to make a fellow sit up.
Such a scramble for the boats, but when we got to our stations
the laugh was on us. We found nothing doing, it was, only
target practice. The boat we were attached to would hold all
but ten men, and they were told off to assist in lowering the
boat, seeing every man safely on board and away from the ship,
then they could look after themselves. Ha! Ha! It reads like a
joke, but is quite true. I was one of the lucky (?) ten, but strange
what discipline can do. We promptly fell in as soon as the
alarm went, and stood by to lower, knowing that if anything
did happen our chances were slim, but each of us had our eye
on some particular loose piece on the deck, ready to fling over
and jump after it, should anything happen; so we felt O.K.

Although in danger every hour, the trip was made quite

pleasant; lots of singing and several boxing matches were arranged. One officer belonging to the Royal Dublin Fusiliers — the right crowd — was certainly the life of the ship. We nicknamed him 'Charlie Chaplin,' for he was such a comic; then we had a Chaplain, a good old sport indeed. The first evening he appeared amongst the boys calling for somebody to sing a song, and soon there was a circle by the hatch, and all hands joining in the chorus. These impromptu concerts were given every evening. On the Sunday evening, the day we arrived in Marseilles, at the usual time, after dinner, along came our Chaplain with the usual smile, puffing away at his pipe and carrying a big book under his arm. Oh, a change this evening, we thought. Being Sunday he is going to tell us about the World, the Flesh, and the Kaiser. He took his old place on the hatch and opening the book nearly took our breath away, when we saw the title on the cover in large letters, "Camp Songs," and our Parson announced that for the opening we would start with "Looping the Loop with Lucy Lou," and we swung along for soldiers are great boys for entertainment, and what splendid singers we find amongst them. There were men there, privates, who had left good positions on the stage, so they made things go along good all the time. We were sorry to part with that clergyman, for he was a real good sort — and as I don't want you to have a hard opinion of him, I may say that after 'Church Parade' on Sunday morning is over that is all that is officially recognized in the Army. For supposing we were on shore, in barracks or camp, when morning church parade is over a man is clear for the day. He can please himself what he does in the

evening, either sing songs, or go to Church, and at Church
Parade that morning this good old Chaplain had a splendid
attendance, and preached a beautiful sermon from the text,
Psalm 23, v. 4.

After landing at Marseilles, we entrained, and after three
days arrived here. The trip was very nice, and the people all
along the route came out, whenever the train stopped, and gave
us tea, cakes, and other comforts. As we glanced out when
going through the different towns and cities we saw enough to
convince us that France has gone into this war with her whole
heart and soul. Not a young man was to be seen, and the only
men we could see were cripples. It was remarkable, considering
the distance we came, (Marseilles to ———, I wonder will the
Censor erase the latter place) not to find even one man of
military age; lots of soldiers shifting to and fro, but cripples
and women doing the work. We saw many women working at
the Round Houses all along the route, some oiling, cleaning,
and doing all sorts or work, formerly — before the war —
done by men, and the tram cars have all women conductors
everywhere in France. And the number of women in black!
What sacrifices France has made, and the half is not told. Some
of the people in London and other places who complain of
zeppelin raids and other things would 'sit up' if they came to
this country and saw French women ploughing in the fields,
scarcely a stone's throw from the firing line.

I have to go on duty now, and as this much will be enough
to make this envelope quite bulky, I shall continue to-morrow,
but one very important thing I wish to refer to before I

conclude, the kindness of those who have sent presents. Some of them I have not traced to the senders, as no letters accompanied the gifts, but I want to thank them just the same.

TWENTY-SEVENTH LETTER.

———

"Somewhere in France,"
April 22nd, 1916.

HEN TELLING YOU ABOUT OUR TRIP from Port Said to Marseilles, I meant to tell you how we were nearly sent to the bottom. On arriving off Malta we were surprised that the ship did not call there. A torpedo destroyer came out and signalled us, and instead of going into the harbour on we went. From what we could find out it appears that a submarine had sunk a steamer close behind us, and of course they thought it safer for us to carry on, than risk entering Malta, which would give the pirate time to come up and wait for us coming out. So away we go, although a little disappointed at not having a few hours at Malta to renew old acquaintances.

Since writing yesterday I have received a lot of letters which have been going all over Egypt, Malta, and England hunting me out, and at last they found me. In one batch I received sixty-eight letters, and they've been coming in smaller numbers ever since. It is so good to get letters after such a long wait. So many have written me from all over Newfoundland, some of them old friends that I hear from regularly, and others from people I have never met. God bless them all; I shall try and reply to every one. How good of them to write, but if they only knew how much a letter — a few kind words of cheer — is appreciated by fellows so far from home, they would be amply repaid. Some friends sent me clippings from the different papers in reference to my letter some time ago regarding shortage of clothing, etc., at Gallipoli. I wish I had heard of this before, but for about four months I have received not a word of news from home, as when a man goes to hospital from Gallipoli he is practically "lost" as regards receiving correspondence. There are so many hospitals in Egypt, Malta and England that nobody knows where he will eventually bring up. Men are moved about from one hospital to another, according to the disease. There is an official record, of course, but it is such a slow 'long-tailed' process that a man may be to some hospital in England cured, and out before he is officially reported so. Accordingly, all the people at home who have had relatives or friends in the Regiment sent to hospital will understand the long delay in getting replies to their letters. I am sorry I did not get any papers, excepting some which were enclosed in envelopes and came as letters. They don't as a rule forward on papers from the Regiment to hospitals. I suppose it makes the mails too bulky, but at the same time there is no place a home paper is appreciated more than when a fellow is lying in hospital.

As I said, I received a few papers and clippings for which I am thankful. I am more than surprised to find that somebody said we had plenty of clothing, etc., on the Peninsula. Is that so? Well it must have been all a dream. Thank goodness there are not many who had the heart to say the boys were grumblers. What a shame; but no doubt they are sorry now. It is such an old story that it is best to let it rest, but I have always tried to steer clear of speaking about our little ills and drawbacks, and only when I was forced to did I mention about the conditions that existed amongst our boys in the trenches. I felt I should say something then of what had been a puzzle to us for months, viz.: What was becoming of all the clothing the W.P.A. and people of Newfoundland were sending to "Ours?" I did it for the best. We all were, and are, thankful to the W.P.A. and good people at home for all they had done — and are doing — for us, but thought some blunders must have been made on arrival of clothing in England, and they were distributed wrongly. A Newfoundland sock is the best in the world and is prized by every soldier. How many times at the Peninsula and before we ever saw Egypt have we been asked by soldiers of different regiments if we had a pair of Newfoundland socks to give them or sell them. They would even offer cigarettes in return. One or two chaps I met at Stob's told me they wanted to get a couple of pairs to send home to their people in England as curiosities — souvenirs —for they could never get the same kind of socks anywhere, and our boys will tell you the same. There is no sock like the Newfoundland home-made sock, so you can just imagine the feeling of our fellows when "dished out" with what is generally known as "Tommy" socks, made by the thousands, the one and only (form number, so and so, regulation, chapter such and such, and so on) knowing that the people at home were sending out thousands of pairs to us. It is only right that anything going to the Regiment for the men should be distributed to them, as the people at home wish. Enough said on this subject at present; I am only glad to let it drop, for I might say something better left unsaid; the thing is over now, and done with, so let it rest.

Amongst the mail matter I received was a package containing copies of Mr. James Murphy's latest songs; they always "take" with our fellows, and I distributed them amongst the boys as far as they would go, but the O.C. here does not know that Mr. Murphy is partly responsible for the singing going on in the Newfoundland lines last night. Those songs always take; the one about the parcels robbed out of the mails took good, and the "Song of the Apples" is a favourite yet. Amongst the nice parcels I have received there are four which I cannot find any account of the sender, probably there are letters to come, but if this should reach the eye of the sender or any of them, I would like to say how much I thank them for their kindness. I hope they will send their names so that I may be able to thank them properly.

This place, as I told you, is close by ———. I cannot say much, as you know it is against the rules, but I feel that there is no harm in saying this place is what its name implies — base — 29th Infantry Base Depot, where troops from everywhere are sent for equipment, before being sent to their regiment. When we got here they put me in the Orderly Room office as they were just opening up a new staff, and for all positions they usually take from the ranks men just out of hospital who are not marked A class. There are 3 classes: A or "Active; T.B. "Temporary Base," (or Temporary Unfit), and P.B., "Permanent Base," (or Permanently Unfit). As my right foot was still giving me a little bother when I came here, the medical officer kept me in the T.B. class, same as when I left Mustapha and Malta. I hope soon to be O.K. again. One lot of our fellows went up to join the Regiment. I hope to get away with the next draft, although I hear that the Regiment is not in the firing line yet, and it is impossible to find out any news of where they are, for they keep things so secret.

Sergeant J. Robinson went with the lot that left. Jack wishes me to remember him to all his friends; he is so well known all over Newfoundland, because so long associated with the City Club and the Coastal boats. Jack is popular with the boys, and liked by everybody. Corporal Jas. Boland came from Ayr a few days ago in charge of a draft of men. Jim formerly worked at the Gas Works in St. John's, and all his friends will be glad to know that he is quite well, and eager for a go at the Germans. I had word from Dan Des Roches of B Company by mail. Dan was then at Cottonera Hospital, Malta, and going on well, but as the letter has been a long time on the road, he is no doubt out of hospital by now. Dan is a genial, good fellow, and thought a lot of in B Company. I hope he'll soon be with us again. Joe Kavanagh went out with the last draft, and whatever car Joe occupies en route the occupants will be kept in good humour, for Joe is a comic and full of life. Lance-Corporal Lewis Bartlett also went, and we all had to smile on board the

Lake Manitoba when the officers were going around asking the usual questions, "In case of emergency, do you know how to row a boat?" etc., etc. When they came to the Newfoundland detachment and asked this question, J. Squires made officers and all roar by saying: "Why, Sir, we got men in this bunch that can lower that boat into the water and pilot her to the North Pole. Don't ever ask Newfoundlanders if they can row or handle anything afloat, for they can build, row and sail them." Lewis Bartlett is a brother of the famous explorer Captain Bob Bartlett, and Lewis is a splendid chap. I wish I could tell you all the curious things that have happened amongst our boys, and our fellows always come out on top.

I suppose you are tired of reading about the deeds at Gallipoli, but strange to say, amongst the different papers I've seen I never happened to see anything in reference to poor Jack Fitzgerald. I know you have had it published, for such a deed as his would never go untold, but one cannot speak too often about a brave deed, and Jack Fitzgerald's was one of the bravest in the whole war, and one well worthy of the Victoria Cross: Poor Jack; he was an excellent fellow, and the morning the others were shot down, he took his Red Cross satchel and went out in the midst of the hail of bullets and began to bandage their wounds. One bullet struck him and he staggered for a moment, and then went on with his work of binding the wounds of his comrade; but shortly after he fell, and when they brought his body in there were five bullets in him. Truly he gave his life for others. Such an excellent character was his, always a pleasant word for everybody; no wonder that the whole Regiment mourned his loss.

TWENTY-EIGHTH LETTER.

———

Somewhere in France,
April 30th, 1916.

E ARE GETTING BEAUTIFUL WEATHER HERE NOW. We often heard of sunny France, but could not understand it at first as it was rainy and cold every day. But the past few days we are getting beautiful sunshine all the day long, and the nights are delightful. It is a wonderful sight here, especially at nights — but mum is the word, some day we will be able to tell you all about it, then there will be no restrictions — no Censors; no shining buttons before going to work; no running at the rate of twenty miles an hour at night to get home so as not to be one minute after 'lights out;' no 'pulling through' a rifle — at the crack of dawn — until she shines on the inside like a new shilling — all over when we get our "civie" clothes on again. I wonder sometimes how we will get into the ways of civil life, and how many blunders we shall make at first after we get home. How many times is a fellow likely to say: "Mother (or Uncle John), has reveille gone yet?" and — delightful to think of — somebody will say: "You are not in the Army now, when you feel like getting up breakfast will be

ready," or "Will you have breakfast in bed?" Oh what a change
— no more "bully" beef or apricot jam; but before that comes,
there is some stern work to be done. Britain is ready, and the
Allies are ready, so there can only be the one result.

One or two in writing me said: "Have you any idea when
this war will be over?" I feel honoured, but can only give the
same answer Kitchener and others are giving, that is: "The war
will be over during the year;" but they don't say WHAT year.

There is a fine picture house here, and nearly every night
some of the films are from "Charlie Chaplin." Have you had
any at home? for they are certainly good. Charlie is the greatest
comic I've ever seen, and such shapes as that man can put
himself in is amazing. Charlie is a great favourite amongst the
soldiers. We had the pleasure of seeing him act in Edinburgh,
and "my word, we didn't 'arf laugh." There is a parody on
"Pretty Redwing" sung about Charlie Chaplin; the chorus is:

> Oh the moon shines bright on Charlie Chaplin,
> His boots are crackin' for the want of blackin',
> And his baggy trousers they want mendin',
> Before they send him, to the Dardanelles.

There is a lot of our old friends, Dubs., Munsters and
Inniskillings here, and amongst the latter I met a young chap
who was at hospital with me at Mudros, (Lemnois). He was in
the next cot to mine. This young chap, his name is Kearley, was
struck just behind the ear and the bullet, or piece of shrapnel,
lodged in his throat. The doctors put him under X-Rays trying

to locate the bullet. Kearley was certainly a patient fellow, but could give the doctors no information to help them in locating the troublesome impediment; he did not know then if it was a rifle bullet or a piece of shell, or shrapnel bullet. They brought in different doctors, who questioned him, and all the information he could give was: "I was in the second line of trenches; I heard a "buzz" in my ears, and when I woke up the Nurse said, 'here try and drink this'." Kearley, like many another, was unconscious until after he got on the hospital ship. I am glad to say he is now fully recovered. They got the bullet out, and it proved to be a shrapnel bullet. You understand what that is; the Turks and Germans, too, have shells filled with small, round bullets — sometimes they put all sorts of things in these shells — pieces of iron, old nails, etc., and on the shell bursting the contents spread all over the place, and a man is lucky to escape if the shell bursts amongst a bunch. I had several narrow escapes from those horrid things, and a shell is so tricky. You sometimes can get an idea where it is going to pitch and can run to cover, other times you hear the whistle, oh, that horrid, ominous whistle, and you wonder where it will strike — in front, behind you, or where? In those cases, you stand still and wait, and your heart goes "pit-a-pat" — oh no, as you were, my mistake, you (what is it the penny dreadfuls tell us?) you fold your arms and look brave and defiant and wonder whereabouts she'll burst. Once, shortly before I went to hospital, six of us went for water one day about 10 a.m., and just as we got near the well we heard the 'whistle.' The Turks were dropping quite a lot of shells that morning, and we were walking along in twos, and when we heard the shell, the awful whistle — "shew-u-u-u," — we stopped; where would she strike? and we heard it getting oh, so close. We stood quite still, no time to look for cover, and waited. Every second seemed an hour. I said to myself I think I'll shut my eyes; — gracious me, one feels so safe with the eyes shut, —then the bang, right at our very feet. Such a bang, if you want an idea of the sound, just press your ear on the 12 o'clock gun and keep it there whilst it is being fired. I waited; I felt myself all over, and said to myself am I here or in the air? So I lifted one foot and put it back again, and felt the solid ground. I am here at any rate. Then I opened my eyes and looked around. I counted six of us still here, and most remarkable, only one man wounded, Arch Newman, of Twillingate, wounded in the hand. I heard he lost two fingers after going to hospital. I think that was a very remarkable escape for us, and then we began picking up souvenirs, Turkish bullets, I have several, picked up at different times.

The Turks had a nasty fashion of finding out the places where we would get water and kept shelling us. You know, of course, water was very scarce on the Peninsula. Now if you are not tired hearing about the Peninsula, I will tell you a bit more, for there are so many little deeds, little incidents that you have never heard. So if you are "fed up" with Gallipoli yarns, I must only ask you to pass this into the W.P.B. Well, I was going to tell you a story about the water, which, rest assured, I would never tell at the time. After the flood, our cooks got some water out of a well we had been using to make tea for breakfast, and we all noticed the tea had a peculiar "flavour" — ahem! —and then on going to draw the water for dinner we discovered where the "peculiar" aroma came from, the bucket struck something hard in the well, and they got ropes, etc., and hauled it up and found it was a dead Turk, who had floated across in the flood, and nowhere else would do him but he had to settle himself down in our well. Ugh! We had only "bully" beef and biscuits and no drink for the rest of that day, and until we had made a new well.

Lew O'Dea no doubt is well known in St. John's, he was on the Police Force for a time. Well Lew is in No. 8 platoon, and I shall never forget the morning he came down through the trench, and somebody "held him up" for a Turk. Lew had lost his great coat, and nothing daunted, had picked off a Turk, taken the coat off him, and put it on. Lew is certainly a "dry chip" and kept everybody in good humour by his quaint ways. He has that coat yet, I daresay, as he intended bringing it back to Newfoundland as a souvenir.

Walter Day is here, and is quite well. He is pretty well known in St. John's; his father works at Gale's Bakery, and if this should be seen by any of his friends they will be glad to know Walter is going on all right. His brother Jim, is also O.K. Peter Bennett, D Company, is here, and is quite well. Harry Thompkinson of B Company left yesterday for Ayr. Harry was wounded in the Dardanelles and on examination by the Medical Officers here they pronounced him P.B., that is Permanent Base duties, not being fit for active service again. Harry deserves the well-earned rest, for he has done his part faithfully and well.

We are all wondering when those chaps at home are

coming out to join us. Surely they will not hang back when so much is at stake. I think some fellows don't realize what it means if Germany gets the upper hand. Are they under the impression it will not affect Newfoundland? But it will; and not only Newfoundland, but the whole world would suffer if such a monster as the Kaiser became dictator over us, but that must not be, so come on boys, "fall in."

TWENTY-NINTH LETTER.

────────

France,

May 19th, 1916.

UST A FEW LINES to let you know we are going on O.K. I am still at the Base; I have to go before another medical board Thursday, then I hope to get marked "fit" and sent with the unit.

We are having lovely weather just now, real summer, and summer in France is ideal. I had a look around Rouen the other day. It is a fine city. I visited the church where the ashes of Joan of Arc (Jeanne d'Arc) are buried, also the tower where Joan was kept a prisoner before being burnt to death. The French to this day think "some lot" of Joan, for numerous monuments and statues are to be seen almost in every public place in memory of this woman who led the French to victory.

Sergeant Gerald Byrne is here from hospital fully recovered. Gerald is one of the best; he is senior N.C.O. in command of Newfoundland details here. In looking over the Newfoundland papers, only lately received, giving details of the work done by our regiment at Gallipoli, C Company gets quite a lot of praise for the splendid work they did at Caribou Hill. I am afraid we are apt to lose sight of the work done by B Company during that trying time, and the arrival of Gerald Byrne here calls to mind the important part he played in that affair. Gerald is just from hospital after recovering from frostbite and chill caused during the Caribou Hill affair and the awful storm so soon after. Sergt. Byrne was in charge of a party of men who went out and took over Caribou Hill the night after it was taken by Captain Donnelly and party. Never a word have we seen in print about Gerald and his men, a band of as true heroes as ever did anything on the Peninsula, but many things have been overlooked in the excitement of the moment, and only after it is all over and we have time to sit down and think, do the many brave deeds performed by our boys come to mind. It is long past now, but "a brave story never dies with age." Let me tell you about it. Sergt. Gerald Byrne in charge of the following men of B Company: Will Cleary, George Knight, Will Melee, Wm. Green and Rhody Callahan, (poor Geo. Knight was afterwards killed), went out to Caribou Hill to relieve Capt. Donnelly's men. He, (Gerald), extended his men along the hill facing the enemy, and at that time our position was not well fortified. It was scarcely dark when they got there, and all suddenly a band of Turks appeared to attempt the recapture of the hill. The Turks sprang up from amongst the thorns and bushes not more than ten yards from Gerald and his men. Instantly Gerald ordered rapid fire, and the Turks followed 'suit.' In the midst of this our boys saw Turks coming up on both flanks, and I can assure you it required some coolness on his part to direct the fire of his five men so as to cover both flanks of the enemy who appeared in large numbers. No doubt the Turks thought we had more men holding them off or they would have rushed our boys. Many Turks fell, but up to then, not one of Gerald's little band was hit. Later on as it grew darker the Turks crept up nearer, and Gerald, on glancing over the rock covering his head, saw a Turkish officer not five feet away and his men hid behind. The Turk took deliberate aim at Gerald, and the bullet skimmed by his ear, as narrow an escape as a man ever had. Billy Cleary, who was next to Gerald almost got it too. Gerald took deliberate aim and shot the Turkish officer who fell at once and the groans of agony from that man were heartrending as he lay mortally wounded. Then the Turks opened rapid fire again, and our boys replied. Many Turks fell; there was scarcely a miss from our men, but luckily none of our chaps were killed. Billy Melee and W. Green were both wounded, but held on and bound their wounds up. There they stayed until relieved at daylight next morning. In the midst of one attack four Turks were close on our crowd and threw several bombs which missed. Then Gerald went to give them a few more shots, also Will Cleary, but unfortunately owing to the rapid fire kept up all the evening and night their rifles "jammed." Will Cleary saved the situation by instantly picking up a couple of bombs and accurately dropped them in the midst of the four Turks, and when Billy Cleary returns to Newfoundland ask him to describe the result of those bombs, for it is a treat to hear him tell how, Turks, gravel and dust went up in the air together. The Turks drew off then, and our boys stayed there in the perishing cold all that night, a night none of them will ever forget, without a particle of shelter. All of B Company were building up sandbags at the back of the hill close by. Little we knew at the time that our six heroes were going through such a fierce time, and yet the rapid fire coming from the enemy was tearing the sandbags open almost as fast as we would lay them down. It was an awful night, and most remarkable no more of us were hit, for the Turks threw more bombs that night than I ever noticed before. I only mention this story now so that the friends of these six men may know that we look on them as heroes, as brave as any men on the Peninsula.

Dick Pittman, (Corporal), is here now, second in command Newfoundland details. Dick is fully recovered from the result of his experiences in Gallipoli. He must have been born never to be killed by bullet, for Dick was in charge of a sandbag party that was building up the firing line the time of the Caribou Hill racket, and once a bullet ripped the peak of his cap. Another time a bomb exploded, and only for the sandbag at his head, Dick would hardly be here to-day. The bag of sand was torn to smithereens and Dick escaped with a shower of sand in his eyes, nose and mouth and down the back of his neck. Corporal Dick Pittman is another of B Company heroes, and everybody ought to be proud of him. No. 389, Charlie Rogers, formerly of Greenspond, is here too. Charlie was with the sandbag party that night and escaped with a scar from a bullet on his left cheek; a very narrow escape. He afterwards went through the storm and the evacuation, and is now out of hospital, not yet fully recovered from the awful exposures of

Gallipoli. He has been in hospital, in Egypt, four months with rheumatic fever, and at the last medical board here the doctors marked him P.B., (Permanent Base). He will likely be sent to Ayr for light duty. No. 129, Bert. Nichol, is not quite recovered yet, and is still kept here at the Base. Harry Wilson, son of Rev. Jas. Wilson, is getting on fairly well, but his leg is not sufficiently well for the doctors to pass him "fit" yet. Mike Bryan, well known as a cabman in St. John's, is still here. Mike is not yet well enough to join the unit, but getting better all the time. Mike Murphy of C Company is getting on, but his eyes are not quite cured, so the medical men have not passed him 'fit' yet. Lieut. Wilfred Ayre passed through here on his way to the unit. Wilfred is liked well indeed by the fellows, and does all he can for the men, and we were all glad to see him.

In looking over the papers, I note some of the boys returned from the front, and what a splendid reception they got. The people at home are not forgotten by the boys, and we greatly appreciate all they have done for us.

P.S. — I hope my next will be from the trenches; then I will be able to tell you some interesting things about "Ours" in Flanders.

THIRTIETH LETTER.

France,

May 30, 1916.

ASSED THE MEDICAL OFFICERS O.K. and am just leaving for the trenches to join the regiment in the trenches. And I can assure you that it is a real pleasure to look forward to the meeting with the "Old Guard" again. In the coming months I hope to send you letters from the trenches from time to time. We are just off, there is now no time for writing. When the order comes to move, correspondence and everything else, except obedience to instructions, must be forgotten for a time.

THIRTY-FIRST LETTER.

In the Trenches,
France,
June 4th, 1916.

ERE WE ARE "AT IT" AGAIN, this time "Somewhere" in France. Arrived here Tuesday from the Base, and I wish I could describe the scenery from ———— to here, it is simply grand. All the beautiful fields laid out so level, and the trees — oh dear me, what am I thinking of, talking about scenery in the firing line? Some of you will be saying: "What lovely times they must be having in the trenches when the fellows can sit down and write home about the scenery in France," but the main thing in going through life is to "keep cool," especially in war, so why not talk about the beautiful places we have been in, even in the trenches. But I know you are not bothered about what France looks like just now, you are anxious to hear how "our boys" are going on.

Well, I arrived O.K. Tuesday, at ———— just —— miles away, and tramped it up here, but Mr. German, just to show there was no ill-feeling I suppose, dumped a big shell on the station just as I landed. I don't know if they heard I was coming or not and meant this as a welcome, but I thought it real mean, for I had done 'em no harm — as yet — and besides I might have been on the spot where the shell dropped; however, I overlooked it for the time, meaning to bring Mr. Hun to account for it later, and we quietly marched away arriving at —————, the billets behind the firing line, just at tea hour. All the boys were just out of the trenches then for a rest, and they were all glad to greet us.

After reporting, we went to our respective billets, there were fifteen of us; I find myself back in old B Company, 8 Platoon, and then I went to look for tea. Sergt. Cliff Jupp, formerly of Knowling's, is Acting Quarter Master Sergeant, and a splendid chap he is, for soon he got us settled down to tea, and a lovely tea it was. As I ate I said to myself surely this cannot be the firing line. Hebe Wheeler, Jack Thompson and Reg Masters are the cooks, and they work like slaves to keep everybody well fed, and there are "no complaints," so no wonder, as I had that grand tea after the long march, I said: "What a repast, can we really be in the firing line?" And then I looked around at the shell torn walls, the torn up ground, and all the havoc wrought by shot and shell, and I said to myself, "Yes, we are," for only a glance would show us some of the results of German "Kultur," to find the villages deserted in some places, and in others a few hanging on within range of the enemy's guns. How dearly we all love our homes, and these poor French people, like us all, feel it hard to leave, so, at the risk of annihilation, they remain and plough the fields — the women, too, God bless them —working in the fields, driving the teams, etc., right in the very jaws of death. These French people have great hope of the British, and they say to themselves: "We will not let the Germans come any further," and sure enough, it is "about turn" Mr. German must take when the Newfoundland boys and the others get properly underway.

Captain Joe Nunns is now O.C. of B Company. He was Lieut. in charge of No. 8 Platoon at Suvla, but his good work has brought him promotion, and he is now Captain in charge of B Company. Lt. Frank Knight is in D Company, another very popular officer. Many changes have taken place since I left the Regiment. Capt. O'Brien is O.C. A Company, and there is no need of me telling you about him, for A Company are simply wild over him. Next to good old Captain Carty, the boys fairly worship him. We hope Capt. Carty will be back with us again soon. How nice it would be, if we had an "all Newfoundland Regiment," with Lt.-Col. George Carty, Officer Commanding.

Our lot have had a few casualties since coming to France, but on the whole have been certainly in luck's way. Young Curnew was killed a little while ago, and the day before yesterday we lost Sergt. Manning of A Company, killed by a bomb commonly called "whizz bangs." They are so nicknamed as there is no explosion in firing them. All one hears is the "whizz" and then the "bang." It is hard to "cover" for these as there is not time like we have with shells. Poor Manning was a very quiet fellow and liked by his men. They all feel his loss very keenly. The Priest and many of the officers attended the service and young Manning was laid away in the midst of many noble and great, poor humble men, who "gave up their lives for their country." And this is war; we never know what the next day will bring forth, nor the next hour, nor the next minute.

Howard Clark got a shrapnel wound in his head, but is back from hospital again. *His steel helmet saved his life.* He is bringing home the piece of shrapnel as a souvenir. Lieutenant Peter Cashin is in hospital with a wound but we are glad to say he is getting on finely, and hope soon to have him back again. The most genial, good-hearted man in the world, everybody is fond of Peter Cashin. Capt. Raley is back again as Adjutant. Capt. Tait is still in hospital. Sergt.-Major Roy Ferguson is C.S.M. of C Company; he is thought a lot of by the boys. Arthur Pratt is now Corporal Pratt, and Acting Orderly Sergt. of B Company. Art is the same genial fellow of old, always the same, and popular with everybody. He went through the Suvla and Cape Helles campaign without a scratch; full of grit. Corporal John Luff is back from hospital hale and hearty. Sergt. Stan Goodyear of the transport department is now Lieutenant. Stan is just as popular as ever. You remember him as our best boxer and wrestler, he is as strong as an ox. Joe Goodyear, another trump, is now Sergeant of Transports. Walter Harnett of the Transports is as jolly as ever; the boys all call him "Boss," he is the boss of his line, and a good chap, too. Bert Dicks is now Battalion Sergt.-Major. Q.M.S. Ebasary has gone away to take a course. Q.M.S. Miles is now Sergt.-Major of B Company. You know Q.M.S. Miles, he is looking after B Company's supplies, and a good man at that. George Butler is now Corporal. George is a sailor, and in fact can do anything, a good all round man. Ern Pike went to hospital for eye treatment today. We will miss Ern, as he is such a genial fellow. Corporal Will Treble is here again, fully recovered. "Billy" is a fine fellow, and everybody likes him. I think he is the coolest man under fire I ever saw, nothing daunts him. Some of the old crowd are still with us in No. 8 and a jolly lot they are, "Bush" Callahan, Fred. O'Neill, Jack Dooley and Larry Hoskins. Larry is always cheerful; we always refer to him as "the man with the smile that never comes off."

The German is a different man from the Turk. Fritz tries to be funny sometimes. On arrival of the Australians in the trenches a notice board went up from the enemy trench, saying: "Welcome Australians, and sons of convicts." When we went up one of them shouted, "Hullo, red men." How on earth they find out things is a mystery to me, but they seem to be aware that Newfoundland was once inhabited by the Red Indian. Amidst the din of battle many things occur, and when I say "din," it is but a small idea of what a bombardment means; those powerful guns all going, and would you believe me when I say the trenches really rock with the concussion? That is the truth, the ground shakes, and we can feel it rock. I will not attempt to describe the noise and din, for I never could. It is better imagined than described, and nobody who has never been through it can even imagine what it is like. Still, in the midst of it all, sometimes we find amusing things occur. For instance, once a message was sent orally by an officer as follows: "Pass the word to Captain ——— to send up reinforcements, but when the message reached its destination it was delivered as "Captain so and so wants you to lend him three and four pence." Well, the Captain didn't get the three and four pence, but the man who bungled the order lost three and four pence and a little more as well the next day.

I will close for this time, but when I get properly underway look out for some interesting letters, as I know you are anxious to know how we are doing.

With kind regards, tell all friends that the 1st Newfoundland are O.K., and never feel downhearted. We will make you all proud of us some day.

THIRTY-SECOND LETTER.

————

France,
June 29th, 1916.

 E ARE OUT TO BILLETS AGAIN FOR A SHORT REST, returning to trenches tomorrow, and then ————, but
never mind that now.

Again our boys have brought honour to themselves and
Newfoundland, but I have no doubt Newfoundland is ringing
from one end to the other with news of the great success of our
raiding party, which under Captain Bert Butler, Lieut. C.
Strong, and Lieut. Greene, D.C.M., played havoc with the
Huns. About fifty of our men made an attack on the Germans,
and although we have to regret the loss of several of our brave
fellows killed and missing, also several wounded, yet the
casualties on the enemy's side amounted to about 400 — score
another for Newfoundlanders. Our chaps are the talk of the
whole line; every man held his life in his hands, and none knew
if they would ever return alive; all heroes as brave as any that
ever went over the parapet. You ought to have heard the praise
given them by the Colonel, also by General Cayley.

Fred O'Neil covered himself with glory, and as a result he
is in hospital with a shattered hand received from a bomb

which was thrown by the enemy and landed amongst them. Fred, without the least hesitation, seized the bomb and threw it back, but it exploded as it left his hand. Although himself receiving a nasty wound his prompt action saved many of his comrades. Jim Murphy also received a nasty wound; also Chas. Butler, Lieut. Strong and Capt. Butler. They say Lieut. Greene's wounds are the worst. We all hope he will pull through, for Greene is a splendid man, a brave man, and has won honours for himself in every undertaking. No doubt you have the official list of wounded and killed, so I had better not comment on it now. Some are missing, we hope they may turn up O.K. Some of them did not turn up until twenty-four hours after the raid. George Phillips of A Company got back next day, "tattered and torn," but what a hero, for George slept in a German dug-out the night before, (cool!), and as far as we can learn the Germans are wondering yet what struck them. Our fellows charged right into their trenches carrying all before them and in a word played "hide and seek" with the Huns, chasing them in and out through the traverses, and dropping bombs on them everywhere. Fully 400 Germans were knocked out by fifty brave fellows. The Germans never want to have another visit from the "White Indians," as they call us; for one day they put up a notice in their trenches, "When are the White Indians from Newfoundland coming over." They know now that some of them have been over, and likely will know more later.

These Germans have a great fancy for putting up messages over their trenches for us to read. One day they put up "We sympathize with you in the loss of Kitchener." We did not know what it meant until that evening the news came to us that Lord Kitchener and Staff were drowned. How strange that the Germans should know about it before we did; but they seem to know everything. No doubt, the sinking of H.M.S. *Hampshire* was planned before she left England.

The other day somebody saw a German digging and fired a shot at him; down drops Mr. Sausage, and held up his shovel signalling the result of the shot, and up he got to dig again, but he didn't signal the next shot — don't ask why!

Captain Bert Butler is a hero, and never daunted. I think he is the bravest man I ever saw; he cares for nothing, and today he is going about, happy as a lark, with a bullet wound in his cheek.

Our bombers have done great work and are ready to do even more when the time comes. Lance-Corporal Arch Gillam is in charge of 8 Platoon Bombers, and he has a good team with him: J. Pennell, F. Freake, T. Seymour, G. Abbott, N. Dean, G. Madore, and last, but not least, the unconquerable Joe Andrews. Joe came out to the Peninsula, and not getting enough of it there, he determined to do away with some Germans before seeing Newfoundland again, and here we find Joe Andrews going about like an armoured cruiser ready for action, and goodness help Germany when he gets going. He is a very accurate shot with bombs and rifle. Joe is also a good singer, and helps to pass many a weary hour when out for a rest.

Did I tell you about the mud here yet? Well, just a word; it is mud and slush from head to toe. We are quite used to it now, and would you believe it, we enjoy it. Yes, it is great fun, for believe me, a man can get used to anything, and when this bunch gets back they will be the hardiest lot of men in the world. Here we face danger, awful danger, every hour, looking over the parapet sometimes during a beautiful clear sky, gazing across "No Man's Land" to the enemy's lines, perhaps at just before dawn. It is wonderful how our boys have hardened to this life — shot and shells — and some shells you bet — flying all around them, yet not a flinch. Ah, I wish I could just, in imagination, take you into the trenches. I wish I could illustrate to you just what it is like, but I cannot. No pen could describe what it is like, how calmly one stands and faces death, jokes and laughs; everything is just an every day occurrence. You are mud covered, dry and caked, perhaps, but you look at the chap next you and laugh at the state he is in; then you look down at your own clothes and then the other fellow laughs. Then a whizz bang comes across and misses both of you, and both laugh together.

Now, just for a minute come into our dug-outs, not the same as at the Dardanelles (oh, that Dardanelles) there we had dug-outs aback of the firing line, here we have some in the trenches. So in we go; I only want to tell you about the rats; they are in swarms, and big monsters. I never thought rats could grow so big, and there we find them roaming about the dug-outs, looking for our rations. They chew our clothes, our equipment, everything they destroy, and roam around the dug-out so cool, many of them bigger than any cat I ever saw, and as we enter they just look around as much as to say: "Oh, so you're back again," and then they go digging in to our iron rations. We chase them away; they go just a little way and stop again, and if you go up and kick them, why they only turn and snap at your boot. They consider themselves part of the establishment, and have come to stay; and when we lie down for a rest we can feel them walking over us in swarms. The only thing is to lie still and let them have their fling, but it nearly drives a man's patience out of him sometimes when he feels a rat's whiskers tickling his ear. They just stroll about on us and calmly look at our shoulder badges to see what regiment we belong. The weather is rather cold at nights, but the beautiful summer will soon begin here.

The other day some of us visited Gus Manning's grave. I am sure his friends will be glad to know that he is not forgotten by his comrades. I think his grave is by far the best amongst that lot of heroes who have died for King and Country. Officers and men from all parts of the great British Empire lie there. I wish I had been able to take a photo to send you, but alas! cameras are not allowed here. At the head of Sergt. Manning's grave is a beautiful cross, standing above all the others, and at first appearance it seems like marble, the work is done so nicely, and is a credit to Gus Lilly and Lew Stone who made the cross and did the painting, with inscription, and on the grave are many flowers, showing the esteem in which Gus Manning is held by his comrades.

Our cooks are still busy on the job cooking under fire, but B Company, at any rate, are always assured of regular meals, while the redoubtable Hebe Wheeler is in charge, for Hebe only laughs at shells; he must bear a charmed life, for he has had many narrow escapes. Only two days ago when they were moving the Field Kitchen across a dangerous place, a shell knocked the cover of one of the boilers off, and at the same time sent Jack Thompson's helmet spinning into the soup; but who minds that, "steel soup" is a change anyhow. Just after that their horse was killed, but nothing daunted, Hebe Wheeler, Reg. Masters and J. O'Driscoll fastened themselves into the shafts and brought the kitchen to safety. These are only some of the many incidents that occur every day. Sometime when we return we shall be able to tell you lots and lots of things that time and circumstances will now allow now.

Now, don't think that although we are here in the midst of the greatest war ever known that we don't enjoy ourselves when we get a chance, for a football match is going on at present just outside our shell-torn billet. We have many pleasant hours by holding impromptu concerts, and some of our chaps are great comedians. Then talking about humour: we will never forget 'Bush' Callahan when he came across a German dug-out filled with Germans. "Rod" knows a few German words, and he sang out, "how many men in this dug-out?" The Germans, thinking, no doubt, it was one of their officers, replied: 'Eleven.' "Then," said "Bush," as he threw in two bombs, (time fuse five seconds), "share these amongst you." Oh, if you could have heard the roar of those bombs in that confined space, the screams of the "baby killers," and the patter of Callahan's feet as he beat a hasty retreat. It was a grand stunt, but "Bush" Callahan thinks that nothing. "Not a bad haul," he said, "eleven at one go."

Captain J. Nunns is O.C. of B Company; Captain Leding-ham O.C. of A; Captain Rowsell of C, and Captain Eric Ayre of D. D Company speak highly of Captain Ayre, who takes a great interest in the men. Captain Rowsell of C Company is just as popular as ever, and Captain Ledingham of A is thought a lot of by his men. Of Captain Nunns, I have already told you.

I will ring off for this time but will write again shortly, when I hope to send you a very interesting letter. Tell everybody that they may feel proud of the Newfoundland Regiment, for we get nothing but praise from the Divisional General down. With kind regards.

THE STORY OF
MAY-O-LINDS

Pte. Reginald Fraser   THE FOURTH SHIPMENT   Petty Officer Warren, D.C.M., H.M.S. Briton

THE MAY-O-LINDS

RIVATE FRANK LIND is known throughout Newfoundland as "Mayo Lind," and the story of how he won the name, is worth telling.

In his letter written from Stob's Camp on May 20th, 1915, are the following words:—"The "hardest problem we have to face is the tobacco; it is almost impossible to get good tobacco in this country. A stick of Mayo is indeed a luxury." It was a casual comment but the inference was irresistible and within a few hours after the receipt of his letter the first May-o-Lind appeal was launched. It was an appeal as well for those who did not smoke, as for those who did, for although there were many of the former in the regiment, it was resolved that to smoker and non-smoker alike, a Mayolind should be sent, as those who did not smoke would find a ready market for their Mayolinds amongst those who did, and the proceeds would find them some more congenial solace.

The first Mayolind appeal was for the Newfoundland Regiment only and for Mayo plugs alone. Its purpose is explained by the following extract:—(*Daily News*, June 7, 1915).

> A "Mayolind means what it implies, not cigarettes, not fancy tobacco, not elaborate packages and pictures, but a square pound of honest Mayo. There is plenty of good

tobacco in England but our boys want the cake tobacco, not the cut variety; the solid article, not the mixture. It is easier to carry, more satisfying, more helpful, more enjoyable and, above all, more homelike. A whiff of Mayo is redolent of Newfoundland. Made in Newfoundland, and the gift of Newfoundlanders, it will come to our Newfoundland boys as a grateful reminder of this dear old Newfoundland of ours and of theirs. Our Navy boys can get cake tobacco regularly. It is unexcelled in quality, and cheap. Our soldiers are unable to buy it at all and a pound of cut tobacco means to them not 40 cents but $1.60.

In the first paragraph of the appeal the keynote was struck in the words: "The essence of the appeal lies in the promptness of the response." This characterized each of the six appeals and on every occasion was the objective attained within the time limit of from seven to fourteen days. The total amount raised in the various appeals exceeded $8,000, but as through the generosity of the Imperial Tobacco Company the tobacco and subsequently the cigarettes were supplied at cost and charges, whilst excise duties were waived by the local Government and customs duties by the Imperial authorities, the spending power of the various funds was increased at least four fold, so that the value of the tobacco distributed, based on retailers' prices in the old country, was between $30,000 and $40,000.

The first appeal was for Mayolinds, that is for pounds of tobacco, forty cents representing a Mayolind. Without solicitation, His Excellency Sir Walter Davidson, K.C.M.G., then Governor of Newfoundland, started the ball rolling. Fifteen hundred were required as six companies were then on active service, and when the list was closed, ten days later, over 1700 had been received. The Imperial Tobacco Company through its manager, Mr. Hawvermale, supplied the 250 Mayolinds for one company, displaying similar generosity on four subsequent occasions.

The Mayolinds were promptly despatched and on July 17th, their receipt was acknowledged by Lieut. M. Frank Summers, Quartermaster of the Nfld. contingent then at Acreknowe Camp at Stobs. Within two months of Frank Lind's letter being written, 1461 Mayolinds had been received and distributed, and as Frank quaintly said in a letter written on July 14, 1915: "It is needless to say I am now called Mayo Lind."

On October 28th, 1915, the second appeal was launched. It was intended as a Christmas message to our lads in Blue as well as those in Khaki. For reasons that it is unnecessary to discuss, these Christmas Mayolinds failed to reach the Dardanelles, and it was nearly midsummer of 1916 before the messages reached the regiment then in France.

The appeal was a splendid success. This time it was not 1500 Mayolinds that were asked for but nearly twice the number. The goal was reached after a brief eight day campaign, and by the *Stephano*, afterwards torpedoed in American waters, 2900 were despatched, 1100 to the Dardanelles, 1050 to the Royal Naval Reservists and 750 to the boys at the Depot in Ayr. To the great kindness of Major Montgomerie of the Furness Withy Line, the donors were indebted for the free conveyance of the various consignments across the Atlantic, and to the Red Cross Line, through Hon. John Harvey, for conveyance to Halifax, where the consignment of the "Christmas Mayolinds" was trans-shipped.

A feature in connection with every one of the six appeals is that from first to last there was no personal solicitation. The contributions throughout came as spontaneous replies to the brief message of Mayo Lind.

It was on November 17th, 1915, that the "Christmas" Mayolinds were despatched, but for many weeks there was silence. Beyond a cable from the commanding officer, presumably Lieut.-Col. Hadow, dated Suez, and reading as follows: — "Many thanks for letter, November 18th, just received. Will advise you as soon as consignment arrives," nothing was heard of the shipment, until on March 24th, 1916, Sir Walter Davidson instituted personal enquiry, when the safe arrival of the ton and a half of tobacco shipped four months previously, was advised; and the following day a letter was received from Quartermaster, Lieut. Edwards, from Ayr, acknowledging the 750 consigned to the Depot.

In April of 1916, Mr. Arthur Steele Maitland, writing to His Excellency, Governor Davidson, asked for tobacco, cigarettes and rifle covers for the Regiment. Thereupon at Sir Walter's request the third Mayo Lind Fund was started, the list being headed by a subscription of $50 from the Governor. This time cigarettes were asked for, and in compliment to Mr. Steele Maitland, whose work in connection with the Newfoundland War Contingent Association was greatly appreciated, the appeal was for "May-o-Linds and Steel-Maitlands." Owing to the incomprehensible delays in connection with the Christmas consignment, the new appeal could not expect to attain the same popularity as the former ones — but happily it did so. This time and thereafter it was not in "Mayolinds" that acknowledgement was made, but in dollars; and when the curtain rang down in a fortnight over $1350 had been subscribed, the equivalent of 3400 Mayolinds. On this occasion 2013 lbs. of Mayo and over 100,000 cigarettes were shipped. A thousand parcels were separately packed, each containing a Mayolind (one pound of Mayo tobacco) and five packages of Gem cigarettes for the boys on the firing line. The remaining 1,000 lbs. and 50,000 cigarettes were sent in bulk, and consigned to the Newfoundland War Contingent Association for distribution at discretion, with the request that preference should be given in every possible case to Newfoundland's sick and wounded sailors and soldiers, to Royal Naval Reservists and to men on furlough. The admirable and prompt manner in which the third and subsequent consignments of tobacco were handled by the War Association merits the appreciation of the donors. It will always be a matter of regret that the Christmas Mayolinds of 1915 were not sent to the Association.

At long last the Christmas Mayolinds reached France. On May 18th, the third consignment left for Liverpool, and on the same day a letter was received from Capt. M.F. Summers, of honoured and gallant memory, from "Somewhere in France." It was some compensation for the annoyance that the delay had caused to read in Capt. Summers's letter the following words,— "they could not have come at a better time for the men are in the trenches and it means more to them there, perhaps, than if they were in rest billets."

The Mayolinds and Steel Maitlands reached the War Association on June 21st and those for the Firing Line were immediately forwarded.

The Fourth May-o-Lind Fund was initiated on Sept. 26th, 1916. It opened with these words: —

> There is a pathos attaching to this fourth appeal, that was absent in the others. Then the cheery voice of Frank Lind spoke through every written line. Today he ranks amongst the missing. And yet the call is just as much Frank Lind's as any of the others. If the first of July, day of heroism and of fate, has stilled the hand that penned so many messages of kindness and so many tributes of praise — the voice is still heard. If Frank is a prisoner in Germany, no greater joy could be his than to know that the Fund, inseparably identified with his name, is being continued. If he has answered the Immortal Roll Call, the best testimonial that can be paid to his memory is to do for our gallant lads on sea and land that which he would most have desired and most appreciated, had he been privileged to still mingle with them as friend and comrade.

This time the appeal was for 2500 lbs. of Mayo and 150,000 cigarettes. The sum asked was $2,000. In eleven days $2,082.34 was raised and the list closed. The response was a graceful tribute of gratitude and appreciation to Private Francis Lind, demonstrating that though his merry voice was stilled and his cheerful pen no more told of matters grave and gay, his influence endured. All the appeals were Frank Lind's but the Fourth appeal was his in an especial degree.

By the *Tobasco* the fourth consignment was shipped on Oct. 19. Before leaving it was photographed with a soldier on one side and a sailor on the other. It consisted of thirteen cases and contained 3,200 cardboard boxes, each containing a pound of Mayo, fifty Gem cigarettes and a Christmas Greeting card with Frank Lind's photograph on the back. The receipt was promptly acknowledged by Mr. Reeve, C.M.G., the honorary Secretary of the Newfoundland War Contingent Association, who on Dec. 7th said that those consigned to the men on the firing line had been despatched and should reach them by Christmas, whilst a brief note from the Rev. Father Nangle, C.F., dated Jan. 18th, 1917, concluded with the words,—"the very welcome gift of 'smokes.' Needless to say they were, as always, heartily appreciated by everybody."

The Fifth appeal was under the name of "Cheero-Linds." Captain Clayton, C.F., in a lecture stated that our boys wanted cigarettes, not tobacco. In view of this and as both tonnage and submarine problems were acute, it was decided to drop the Mayo tobacco and send the cash to the War Contingent Association, to be expended on tobacco, chocolates, etc., in such way as was deemed to be best. There was then a balance in hand of $249. For the first time the appeal dragged a little, the omission of "Mayo" apparently not being approved. However in about a fortnight the objective was reached, and a draft for $1551.87 was sent to Mr. Reeve, C.M.G.

The final appeal at the end of March 1918 struck a new note. At a meeting of the War Contingent Association held on March 6th, requests from Newfoundland prisoners of war in Germany for home tobacco and cigarettes were discussed and the promoters of the Mayo-Lind Fund were asked if it were not possible, despite tonnage troubles, to send a consignment. Of course there could be only one reply to that, and immediately 160 boxes, each containing 4 plugs of Mayo and 50 Gem cigarettes, were sent by parcel post. Then came the closing appeal and right willingly was it answered. Over $1500 was raised in a fortnight and 3,000 May-o-Linds despatched. Later 50,000 cigarettes were sent for the sick and wounded in hospitals and the balance of the fund, $67.02, was passed to Mrs. Emerson, Hon. Secy. of the Women's Patriotic Association for use in such manner, consistent with the object of the fund, as might be considered best.

The accounts of the six appeals were audited by Mr. W.L. Donnelly, the assistant Auditor General, and duly published.

The total raised was as follows:—

Midsummer Mayo-Linds, 1915	$ 680.10
Christmas Mayo-Linds, 1915	1033.95
Mayo-Linds and Steel-Maitlands, 1916	1278.55
Christmas Mayo-Linds, 1916	2082.34
Cheero-Linds, 1917	1360.63
Victory Mayo-Linds, 1918	1807.80
	$8243.37

An analysis of the disbursements will be of interest to the many subscribers of the funds. Through the generosity of the steamship agents, freight charges were eliminated. Insurance, light at the first shipment, became with each shipment increasingly heavy, because increasingly necessary. The item of packing was for Gallipoli, tin boxes, heavily lined, being considered necessary. The hope is that the boys in France found some use for the cases. The postage was to cover the 160 Mayo-Linds hurried off by parcel post for prisoners of war. Forwarding charges are those of the Liverpool agents by whom the consignments were sent by rail to London.

Amount expended in Tobacco	$8019.31
Insurance, Job Bros. & Co., Ltd.	133.33
Packing (Gallipoli)	25.00
Forwarding charges, R. N. Morgan & Co. .	56.80
Postage of 160 Parcels	7.68
Cable	1.25
	$8243.37

Thus out of every dollar collected, only 23/4 cents were disbursed for expenses, leaving 971/4 cents expended in tobacco and cigarettes.

Index

157